"A first class primer for the actor. Precise, and amazingly compact."
— Dugald MacArthur, *Professor of Theater and Head of the Professional Actor Training Program, Temple University*

"Not just another acting book, but a true, applicable actor's handbook."
— J.C. Svec, *Director of Theater Operations, Rutgers University - Newark*

"Through this book, beginners will be well on the way to understanding how to develop a character, while experienced thespians will find useful details about technique. . ."
— *School Library Journal*

"Jeremy Whelan's Tape Technique has unlimited potential. It works. . . I endorse this book without reservation. It will be my standard text on acting for a long time to come."
— Mel Shrawder, *Head of Performance, Department of Theatre Arts, University of Miami*

"One of the best practical acting manuals. The Whelan Tape Technique is superb in its simplicity and helpful to the actor regardless of level."
— Stanley Wilson, *Producer, Covert Productions*

"I am thrilled with Mr. Whelan's *ABC's of Acting*. It totally covers the needs of the student."
— Bonnie Cowlishaw, *Program Coordinator, Video and Film Production, Orlando College*

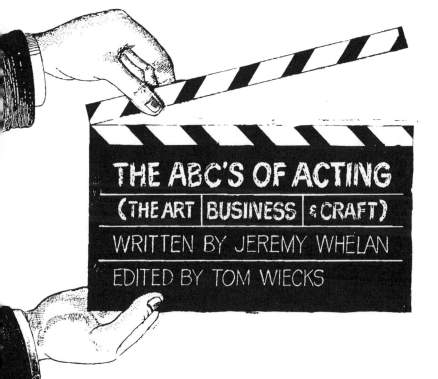

THE ABC'S OF ACTING
(THE ART | BUSINESS | & CRAFT)
WRITTEN BY JEREMY WHELAN
EDITED BY TOM WIECKS

A big thanks to David Forester, Jay Fraser, Joel Grayson, Karen Lever, Julie Nolton, Janice Reinmiller, Hilary Russell, Vance Smith, Jamie Wiecks, Sarah Wiecks and Barbara Williams.

Published by Grey Heron Books
290 S.W. Tualatin Loop
West Linn, Oregon 97068

International Standard Book Number 0-935566-26-0
Library of Congress Catalog Number 89-091818

Cover design © 1990 by Tom Wiecks
Manufactured in the United States of America

This book is dedicated to Lee Strasberg, Viola Spolin and to my friend and daughter L.A.

Table of Contents

PREFACE

One of the hardest things for the beginning actor to understand is it's ok to take acting seriously, it's an honest job. It's as much a job as being a lawyer, a corporate executive or a pick and shovel laborer. Serious, brilliant men and women have dedicated their lives to its study. Once you get past the glamour and romance of it, once you realize that you still have to feed the kids, pay the mortgage and do all the things in life that demand money, then you realize that it's not a game, it's a job.

Yes, it is an art, but you've got to fight hard for your chance to be brilliant. A good "bread and butter" actor can make more money on an hourly basis than the president of many good-sized corporations. So take it seriously. You don't get that kind of money without working for it.

One more thing. Early in my career I was doing a lot of hot shows "off Broadway," and sometimes people would come up to me to talk about "work" or commercial representation and I would look down my nose at them and say, "I don't do commercials."

Well, now I think that if you're an actor and can make your living as an actor, you're one of the luckiest people in the world.

— Jeremy Whelan

ON PROFESSIONALISM
IN ACTING

Ultimately, professionalism is what keeps getting you jobs. It's the actor who is always on time, always does his homework, analyzes the script and has the ability to take direction who works—again and again.

A hard-to-work-with actor is generally unemployed. Film shoots can cost thousands of dollars a minute, so you want someone who gets the job done. If an actor holds you up for an hour by being late, being difficult with wardrobe, make-up or hair, or because of problems with drugs or alcohol, he or she is ripping into your schedule and forcing you over budget. If there is no more money, you may have to sacrifice in other areas, areas you felt were important to the production. In the worst case you may have to close down a production, unable to finish, because of the unprofessionalism of one actor. No producer can afford to gamble like that, and the ones who do regret it. So the problem actor is out. In 99% of the cases nobody will touch them. What good is it to be a great actor if you haven't got an audience?

So *always be professional.* If you have a class and can't make it, be sure to call. If you're going to be late, call. If you've scheduled a rehearsal with anyone and you can't make it or you'll be late, call. Build professional habits *right now*. Professionalism is a state of mind. Get into it. Approach every part as if it were Academy Award time.

Do the best work you can do in workshops. I pound this in every time. Rehearse, rehearse, rehearse! I was very gratified when one of the actresses in my workshop came in with a t-shirt that said, "I can't, I've got to rehearse." Be proud of your professionalism, guard its reputation. Build its reputation—start right now! You'll get where you want to go much quicker with it and nowhere without it.

If this book ended right here and you truly read and understood everything up to this point and then worked to be 100% professional in everything you did that related to acting, you would be a *working actor!*

You can be a working actor with very little talent. But that is not enough for anyone reading this book because you want to be a star—big star, tiny star. And of course, a great actor. So to do that, you need technique. In the following pages, I will deliver to you enough techniques that if you master them, you will achieve that lofty ambition.

I say deliver because some are mine, some come from great teachers I've had. Viola Spolin and Lee Strasberg are foremost. Others come from other teachers and some from throughout the history of acting.

With these tools in place you can start your real education as an actor. This takes place in the theater, on the sound stage, on location—out working with the pros.

Work hard on your part. It will probably be small at first, but keep your eyes and ears open and ask questions whenever you can without disturbing somebody's work.

CHARACTER IS ALL

ince you are probably learning in a stage environment, these thoughts are related for the most part to the stage. However, the truest truth is that acting is acting—Shakespeare, commercials, sit-coms—it's all acting. The better actor you are, the better you will be in any medium.

The continuity of character an actor learns from stage training is the best preparation for any acting job he or she may be called upon to perform.

In film and television, you will seldom if ever get to perform in continuity. But if you have rehearsed that way, it will be easier to break it up and shuffle it around.

If you're in character, you can never make a mistake.

ON ACTING WITH
THE WHOLE BODY

ords lie. She says, "I hate you," she means, "I love you." He says, "No," he feels, "Yes."

Without the rest of the human apparatus, direct communication is impossible. A phone is a voice hint, but without the eyes, the head, the arms, the legs, the coloring, the smell, the taste, the touch of their skin, it's hard to play a love scene or any scene that will be interesting to an audience. You have to be believable and by profession you must be somebody other than you. Smell, think, taste, touch as they do. That is hard but very gratifying when you pull it off.

Observe someone who is really exhausted. Does he have to say, "I'm tired"? When he does say it, that quality is in the voice but he has already told you quite plainly with his whole body.

When babies are hungry or wet and uncomfortable, they scream with their voices but they also thrash their legs and arms, their heads flop from side to side, their torsos twist. In other words, they tell you with their whole bodies that something is wrong. They don't have *words* to lean on. If you watch mute lovers, they haven't any *words*, but they say as much as they can with their whole bodies. They can be very expressive with postures and looks.

In the way that a blind person develops a very keen sense of hearing, as an actor you must be very conscious of acting with the whole body. However, since you are being someone else whose mode of expression will differ from your own, you will not have that natural psycho-physical synthesis, that automatic spontaneous adaptation of the body to the feeling. So you must create it, in the toes, the back, the elbows and the neck. In other words, *the whole body.*

Concentration is the key here, that and trusting the mental, emotional and body memories. Research *body language.* Research it in your local library, and in your everyday observations of people being people. Only then, break the rules and find a new way to "say it." Make it specific and unique. No cliches, please! Do the research first and use it as something to build on. Extend it, contract it, exaggerate this or that aspect of it. Reach and explore.

Your body language is half of the physical tools you have as an actor.

ON VOICE

he body is the physical manifestation of all our internal sensitivities: emotions, thoughts, health. The voice defines the state of these activities to others. Does it quaver? Crack? Is it harsh? Racked with sobs? Filled with laughter? Soft and loving?

In life we have one voice. As an actor, you will need a greater vocal range. The result of having one voice in life is that we only develop one set of muscles. When our voice changes during puberty, the voice settles, so to speak. Most people use only those muscles for the majority of their life, until it "changes" again in old age. In other words, the voice settles and most people settle for what they get. Others—singers, actors and anybody else who wants more—*work on their voices.* They build other muscles in the throat to produce a more pleasing sound.

We hear ourselves much, much more than we see ourselves. There is nothing that ties us more to ourselves and our own lives, our own problems, our own conditioned reaction to things and people, than our voice. Even when we talk to ourselves, we talk in our same voice. The same rhythms, style, everything. Consequently, a vocal characterization is one of the best things you can do to break away from yourself and enter into somebody else: your character.

Actors must have a good vocal range. It can be the starting point or the finishing touch to a great character.

Exaggerate wildly with vocal characterizations in rehearsal. Use different voices for different emotions: accents, stutters, lisps, anything you can think of. Don't worry about how good your Chinese accent is. Just play them all.

It does not matter what voice you use in performance. The discoveries you make with your vocal exercises in rehearsal will stay with you.

Many scenes and plays have a line that gives us difficulty. Explore such a line over and over, saying it throughout your physical warm-up (next chapter). The contortions of the body exercising will automatically alter the color and tone and volume. Quite often this will provide the key to the proper intonation of the line.

Work on the voice. It is the other half of the physical tools you have as an actor. Play with your voice.

I have seen more of my students make the breakthrough to real acting through voice characterization than any other single technique. Just the willingness to play with your voice is a very large step to more creative thinking for many people.

A regional accent is a hachet in the heart of your ambition. I'm not saying you can't work if you have one—many actors do. But if you're too lazy to do the work necessary to broaden your vocal range, you are limiting the number of roles you can play. You don't have to lose your accent—it is another tool you can use as an actor.

Rip yourself away from yourself. Change your voice for parts.

I had a student who had this great voice—real deep and resonant. He's fiftyish and his posture was slumped. His partner had a very high voice. We had worked on their scene for a while, and it wasn't working. So I told Frank to talk in an unnaturally high voice and I told Dick to force his voice down as far as possible. What happened amazed the whole workshop. In the first few seconds, Frank's posture started to change—the stomach came in, the shoulders squared, and as he continued to talk in that high voice, his posture moved to perfect, his movements had strength and purpose and his gestures had meaning and power. The man was standing up straighter than he had in years—I'm sure of it. In real life he had centered his masculine personality in his voice. So when he had to relate to the world without it, he was automatically transformed and we had a scene. They dropped those voice characterizations and did the scene again immediately, and the discoveries stayed in the body and the problem was solved.

Another example. I was directing a play in Los Angeles and one of my leads was playing a 30 year old virgin male who is seduced by a Hollywood actress. The actor playing the virgin was not getting the change from before and after his deflowering. I knew what I wanted when he came out of that bedroom door after the first time—and it wasn't there. So I broke the rehearsal and told them all to have at least two different voices to use the next rehearsal. The next day the actor played the scene with a weak effeminate voice up to the seduction but when he came out of the bedroom, he did a perfect John Wayne imitation. Again posture followed voice and the shy, frightened little mama's boy was transformed into the proud strutting "Duke Wayne." My man was a hero. I loved it. We dropped the vocal characterizations again and the scene now had life and feeling.

Have fun with your voice.

ON THE IMPORTANCE OF PHYSICAL WARM-UP

our body and your voice are the only two physical tools you have to work with as an actor. You must treat them with great respect. An opera singer would not think of walking on stage unless he or she had done serious vocal warm-ups. A ballerina wouldn't dare go on stage unless she had done a complete body warm-up. As an actor, how can you approach a part, a character, without the same respect for your instruments: your body and your voice?

In the course of performance, you will hopefully receive a genuine creative impulse, something totally honest in character, a moment of pure inspiration. Usually we move through a part on a pure line of technique and talent, but those moments of total creative imagination will come. These are those magic bits of time that we remember, and everyone who sees them remembers them all their lives. These are the payoff for all the hours of working on technique and talent expansion. These are the trophies of our art and they are to be highly respected and loved. We must never, through laziness, miss the opportunity to taste them fully and completely. To do so would be a travesty, a bad joke on everything we say we work and stand for, a betrayal of art and self.

Let us say that you are doing a performance and you've been proceeding nicely on technique and talent. The audience believes you and trusts you. They are relaxed and accepting the things you say and do as an honest representation of the character you are portraying.

From who knows where comes that prize, that moment of brilliance, pure inspiration. You are standing and the Muse says, "Drop immediately into a kneeling position." You drop and every heart in the audience drops with you. They are enchanted, enthralled, and are now more united with you than before. They are now passionate in their belief in you. Their openness to you is boundless and everything you do is now past interesting. They are fascinated. This is the good side of the equation.

Now let us say that everything has proceeded as in the above up to the point where inspiration strikes, except this time you have not warmed up physically. When the inspiration explodes in you, you hesitate. You are not sure if you drop the way the Muse says, you will land the way you are supposed to because you are unsure of your body's ability to respond—you might wind up on your butt and ruin the performance.

So you struggle for the moment and try to get back to technique and talent to continue your now broken line. But what has happened is that you have lost the audience. They had been watching closely and they saw your moment of doubt. They realized that an actor had been tricking them and they resent it. Now they are not open to you. They don't believe you anymore. You may get them back on your side, get them back to believing you again, but you will have to work very hard and it will take time and it will never be as good because somewhere in the back of their collective mind, they don't trust you. It's like betraying a lover—he or she may take you back, but it's never the same, it's never as good.

The same thing can happen with your voice. An inspiration to scream might be blocked out of fear that the voice would crack and it would come out more like a squawk, and you would appear ridiculous. So you negate the impulse, and the scenario above is duplicated.

IMPULSE IS ART. Follow it blindly in rehearsal—discipline it in performance—but never negate it. It takes so much energy to negate creative impulse, you'll look spastic in the effort and audiences that pay good money so they can pretend your performance is reality, not theater (it's called "the suspension of disbelief"), will no longer be with you. Knock them out of the suspension and they hate you. Impulse is a gift.

Audiences pay to pretend your performance is reality

So you *must* warm the body and the voice before *every* rehearsal and *every* performance!

Warm-ups can be of any sort that give you confidence your instrument can respond instantaneously to an inspiration within the physical and vocal capabilities of your character.

While doing your warm-up, be careful. For, when inspired, many people can respond way beyond their normal capabilities. We have all heard at one time or another about the mother who picked up an automobile that was crushing her child, or people who survive long falls from aircraft, etc. So always go a bit beyond what you feel are the physical and vocal limitations of your character in your warm-ups.

It may not be immediately obvious how this relates to film acting, where you can shoot another take and then kneel or scream at that time.

However, it doesn't work that way. Inspiration can not be repeated on cue. We are talking about very special moments in an artist's career. If your body and your voice are warmed up, you've a much better chance of catching those lightning bolts—and I can tell you, they are really sweet.

ON GIVEN CIRCUMSTANCE

went to a Picasso exhibit, and there were some preliminary sketches that he made for one of his famous paintings. They started with a complete drawing of a woman, and each of the succeeding 200 drawings subtract elements of this person until she is finally represented by just a few essential lines.

As actors, we start with those few lines: *given circumstance*. The concrete things that the writer gives us about our character—he or she dresses sloppily, talks too loud, has vertigo, has a hand missing, always carries a gun, whatever—from these few lines we must do the reverse of the great painter and add to the character. We must add step by step, piece by piece, line by line if we are to be great actors.

Character is the ability to understand another person, to penetrate beyond his daily mask. Fall in love with your character! He or she is your new love. The big one. You are curious about everything they say, do, think and feel. They pop into your mind at all times of the day and night. Someone walking down the street with the slightest resemblance will bring them quickly to your mind. Your heart will beat wildly. You will check their appearance, the way they wear their hair, their clothes, how they walk, smile, use their eyes, what catches their attention—everything observable about them. You know what they say but you haven't learned to "read" them yet, to know when something is bothering them, as you can with certain friends and family members.

To help you get to know them, the writer has provided many clues, i.e. *given circumstances.* The script will *tell* you many things about the person, this love of yours.

Read it the way you would a letter. Read between the lines. Look for every little clue that will help you understand them, to know them, what kind of person they are, their morals, their likes and dislikes, their education, their family life, where they grew up and how. Investigate.

First, if you are a student doing a scene from a play or film, you must *read the whole script.* Suppose you pick a scene between a guy and a girl on a bridge. They are simply talking about the day's goings on. If you have not read the whole script, you would not know that twenty pages before she had talked to him about her vertigo, that she said, "Joey, you know I'm petrified of heights." You couldn't know that although they are just talking, she is inwardly terrified and may be fighting with all her might to keep from screaming. You would not know that he told her five pages ago: "Dee, you say you love me. You say you trust me. Your fear of heights is unnatural and if you love me you will walk across the bridge tonight." You also might not know that she said to her girlfriend two pages before, "Oh, no, Marcia, I've got a date with Joey tonight and I just got this pimple on my nose. I'm going to be so ugly. I just want to die." Now she's worried about being ugly and worried about flipping out—this is a complex emotional state. In other words, if you have not read the whole script you will not have all of the important given circumstances to work with. You might make some *choices* about what that person is really going through, but even if the choices you make are great dramatically, you will not be playing *what the writer wrote*. You will not know what the writer needed from the scene to make it fit with all of the other scenes in the piece.

As a professional, your first obligation is to the script. Read and make a list of all given circumstances that illuminate your character. If it says you are a cripple and you walk with a limp, then you *must* do that. When you make a list of all given circumstances you will have a sketch of your character, the bones of the skeleton. When you know everything that the writer gave you, you will also know what the writer did not give you. Now you can use your creativity, your talent to put the veins, muscle tissue and organs on the bones of the skeleton. That is *your job* as an actor.

Until people send you scripts because you are such a "big star," most of your auditions in film, stage and commercials will provide you with three pages, more or less, and maybe a couple of words from the director about the character. This is all you will have, and maybe 15 minutes if you are lucky, to absorb and dramatically interpret *a whole life*. There is not much to go on, and competition is fierce for every role in the professional world. So give yourself every break you can. Do this by establishing good solid professional habits of work right now. Mining your script for all given circumstances is one of the most basic of the professional habits. How could you do a part without using given circumstances? They will help you in two ways. One, when you get a part and a whole script, you will know how to approach it. Two, if you have trained yourself in these methods, when they give you those three pages all given circumstances will pop off the page at you like blinking neon. Your instrument will make the adjustment and your audition will be better, maybe good enough to be better than all the others who auditioned. Good enough to get the part—that is the name of the game.

Just to pound it home with one more analogy—if you don't know the whole play, you don't know the given circumstance. You can't pluck a scene out of a vacuum. The play or film is a piece, a work, a *totality*. It has many of the qualities of a musical work. If the drummer decides to play loud at soft parts, or soft at loud parts, in the former he loses the ensemble, and in the latter he loses himself. Either way, he kills the piece, and it's hard to come out looking good when you do that.

If you're supposed to scream in a scene, and you haven't read the play, you might scream as loud as you can. So when you discover that three pages later it says, "Screams twice as loud," you realize that you violated the text and that you were like the drummer above—not a good feeling. What you did was not in harmony with the rhythm of the scene, and cannot sound correct. Now if you know that you die on the next page, you can blow the roof off the place with your scream and be cool. Always remember the music of it.

ON EMOTION

ach of us possesses the full spectrum of potential emotional sensation. In life situations, the automatic synthesis of body, mind and heart makes our actions and reactions to any given circumstance coordinated. This coordination allows a truthful expression of our innermost sensations.

As a character, however, we must like athletes train that coordination, practicing and rehearsing that activity into harmonious motion and expression.

Why are some people dull, boring and no fun to be around? Usually it is due to the fact that they have a limited emotional vocabulary. Although they are born with the capacity to express the full range of human emotions, they have for whatever reason chosen to exhibit only a few. "Jack is a grouch." "Everything is a joke to Jane." "Jill is always sad." Etc., etc.

These people have short-circuited themselves in life and generally we find them boring. This is not to say that they do not feel the variations of emotion. It's just that they don't express them. If you had to play one of these characters, you would, for the sake of being interesting dramatically, find ways to show that they did feel emotions but that they just did not express them. Unless these people are psychos, that would be the truth.

Question: How do you show someone not expressing emotions they are feeling?

Answer: By showing that person, in the choices they make, suppressing that emotion or emotions.

If you are feeling something that you are not expressing, then you are suppressing it. Dramatic choices can now be made, for the situation has gone from passive (non-expression) to active (suppression). This is a common acting problem. A writer writes a passive situation. The actor must make it active by seeking its *opposite*.

How do we, as actors, learn to portray all the subtle shadings of the human emotional catalogue? Obviously, we must first know what they are. In life, as I have said, this knowledge is both automatic and learned. Conditioning is what throws the spotlight of selection from this choice to that one in each individual human being. Since you are not yourself when playing a character, you must discover. Using given circumstance and imagination, find the answers. Which of that vast range of possibilities would your character choose?

It's something like a juke box. Which buttons will he/she push? Sad song, funny song, sexy song, sentimental song, etc. As people, we do not necessarily know the name of a subtle variation of an emotion which we may be experiencing or expressing. We just do it. It's automatic and it can be a very delicate shade of that emotion, so delicate that it fascinates the beholder, the audience.

A chef must know all of the ingredients in a recipe in order to create a great meal. We, as actors, must know the name of an emotion and all of its ingredients if we wish to recreate it.

In order to know all of these variations, we must study them. An excellent source for building this vocabulary is a thesaurus. *Get one!* Take broad emotional categories: love, hate, fear, joy, etc. and look them up. You will find ten or twenty words which are an aspect or another degree of that emotion. Make a list in ascending or descending order of intensity. Look them up in a dictionary. Write their meaning next to them. Try to picture a situation in which you have expressed or experienced that emotion. You will be, in effect, programming your actor's instrument with its most valuable information. You will be stretching your emotional awareness, giving yourself a much greater selection of possible choices.

Imagine a painter who did not know colors. Painters study all colors and then "invent" new ones. Ask an art student how much time he spends studying color. *Emotions are to actors what colors are to painters.* Study them! Half the problem of acting is being able to recognize the problems of acting.

While in the Air Force, I was joy riding in an old plane. I didn't feel like hooking up my parachute—it

Emotions are to actors what colors are to painters

seemed like a hassle. The captain said, "OK, Jer, but we're at 10,000 feet and heading for 20. If this baby goes down, she goes like a rock and you're not gonna be able to get that thing on." I thought for a very brief second and said, "OK, how do I do it?" The time to learn is now. I was caught up in the excitement of flying and did not want to take time to learn something important, something that was important to my survival. What I'm telling you here is important to your survival as an actor. Take the time and learn it now.

Emotions are to actors what colors are to painters. Learn them from a book—a thesaurus.

Exercise

Go into an artist's supply store or your library one
day and pick up a few books on color. See how
involved it is, how detailed, how explicit. You're an
artist. You have to study, too. You have to study
emotions.

Think of an ice cream parlor with only chocolate
and vanilla. See yourself standing there making
your choice. How long does it take, how much
thought is involved? How interesting is it? Now
picture yourself with 31 flavors spread out before
you. All the colors, all the exotic names. Now how
much thought is involved? How much more
interesting are the choices you can make? I use an
ice cream store as an example because I grew up in
one. We had candy, too—same thing. Apply it any
way you like: a dress shop with only two dresses, a
bar with 200 beers from all over the world, whatever
you have to use to get the idea. The broader your
range of choices, the more interesting your selection.
Get a thesaurus; look up the words in a dictionary.

Build your emotional vocabulary!

You might say OK, I wrote down, studied,
learned every emotion in the universe, but how do I
express them? Well, unless you're playing a carrot, I
suggest that you do it physically, through
movement. Now, this can be a 10 foot running
somersault or a slight twitch of a finger or the
tiniest movement of the eyes, but movement—
internal or external—derived from the line.

ON MOVEMENT FROM THE LINE

hat you need to know about acting and movement is that the motivation is right there in the line. It is what you say that makes you want to move toward or away from somebody, or even stand still. What another actor says to you, about you, or even does not say to you will also make you want to move toward or away from them, or, again, to just stand still.

What you need to know is that a line will:

Repel you away from that person ("John, put down that knife!"). You feel fear, disgust, distaste.

Impel you toward that person ("That looks like my mother's ring."). You feel impelled to get a closer look—curiosity, affection, concern.

Compel you to stand still ("One move and you're dead!"). A command, confusion, indecision.

It's all there in the lines and the way you make that move is all a part of acting, or being somebody else. The style of that movement is up to your creative imagination and the given circumstance of your character. A line given by a crippled vet would demand a much different movement than that same line given by Superman. In both cases, using the same words, the movement is totally different.

With all these things swirling through your head and body, as you try to grasp a character, you can overlook the obvious even if you're a strong actor. But even if you hit all the obvious movements, you still haven't got a performance. It's the subtle, delicate movements that set the fine performance apart. Who wants to go see an actor who is obvious and predictable? The obvious movements must be there because they're obvious and an audience would resent it if they were missing. But it's all the little ones that you, the artist, discover that thrill them and make them want to pay to see you again. So, look at every line and ask your character, does it:

- Repel me away?
- Impel me toward?
- Compel me to stay where I am?

At the highest and the most necessary refinement, this movement can be internal and external, only internal, only external, or any combination.

Example

Repelled Internally—Impelled Externally
You're reassuring somebody you're conning of your sincerity by moving closer to her. Inside you're saying, "My God, I've got to touch this pig!" But outside you're saying, "Darling, I promise I'll give you back the money by Tuesday."

Internally and Externally Impelled

Your lover arrives on a train. You find her in the crowd. She waves, you light up inside. Your insides move toward her and externally your body rushes to wrap itself around her, sincerely.

Internally Impelled and Externally Compelled

You're having an affair with someone. You're in love. Your lover arrives for dinner with his mate at the same restaurant you're in. Your eyes meet. You're impelled to rush over and kiss him, but any sign might give you away. You're compelled to stay where you are, to be discreet. Being compelled to stay still is not passive waiting. It is an active (acting) state.

You're at a dinner party, and you are faint with hunger. (Physical involvement, mental involvement). Food is everywhere, but the hostess is not yet seated. You're not just waiting, you're fully involved on every level, wondering, "Where is she? Why doesn't she get here?" (Emotional involvement). You're angry at her for not being there, and frustrated by etiquette. So even though you're sitting dead still, a million things are happening inside of you. Think of other examples. Imagination—work it!

This sets up the tension.
This is drama.
This is acting.

Repelled—Impelled—Compelled. Let's call it RIC for short. It's there in every line. Look for it, find it, then express it creatively with your own uniqueness, your own talent.

THE WHELAN TAPE
TECHNIQUE

ow this is hot—you can get a long way in a hurry with this one!

After you've read your script once and have gotten an idea about character, sit down with your scene partner and read the scene aloud. Tape it with a small recorder, and rough out the setting with any props at hand. Then get up, start the tape and while you listen, move through the scene making eye contact and physical contact with your partner and the setting, the environment. Don't move your lips. React to the tape. Let the contact flow in any direction it wants. Listen to your own taped voice. Listen to your partner's taped response. Contact your partner—eyes, hands, feet, with objects. Keep that contact all the way through—don't break it for any reason.

As you hear your scene partner say his lines, ask yourself, "How do I feel when I hear that?" When you hear your own voice, ask yourself, "How do I feel when I say that?" When you contact that feeling, it will supply the RIC (see previous chapter).

When it's over, you will have made many discoveries because of the contact. You will have found, or will have begun to find, movement.

Now go back, sit down, and tape it again. A certain life will be in the lines this time. Some variations from how you read the line before will come into the voice because of the contact. You're well on your way to building your relationship with your character, your partner, and your environment.

Don't worry about memorizing lines for now. You haven't got your character yet, so you don't know how he or she will say them anyway. And besides, the mechanical part, memorizing, is already happening when you read it for the tape, when you're moving around freely without books. Scripts in hand at this early stage kill relationships and destroy movement. As you are listening to your scene playback, it's going into your mind on its own. By absorbing the relationships, you make the lines go in that much harder, stronger, better.

With this tape recorder approach, you are not breaking up the process of acting. You are integrating it all immediately, and spontaneity can really kick in. Working this way, you will discover movement through contact with fellow actors and the inner and outer environment. This spontaneous, natural, organic movement through contact will let the lines slip naturally and comfortably into the mind and body far, far more creatively than sitting stupidly at a table doing dull rote, repetitious memorization. You need only to try it to know for yourself.

I invented this exercise while directing a play in Los Angeles in 1985. I am thrilled at its success. It is being picked up and used by other directors around the country.

The tape technique helps replace dull, rote memorization

It is invaluable, and I believe it will revolutionize rehearsals all over the world. Any actor who has had to go through the old stumbling-around-with-book-in-hand routine will immediately feel the exhilaration of discovering movement naturally. Characters develop quickly and relationships form almost automatically. Remember:

Repel—Impel—Compel.

When you get these impulses during a tape rehearsal, make them BIG. Don't worry about how they fit, just make them bigger than life.

During a workshop in Portland using the Whelan tape technique, a student felt repelled by a line her scene partner delivered. She let it throw her away as if a bomb had blasted her. Afterward, we found that she could fulfill that impulse if she moved quickly upstage to get a frying pan (she was cooking in the scene). The movement changed, but the truth of the impulse (totally repelled) stayed through every performance. Let your body experience the initial impulse fully and completely when it happens, and then work it into the scene later.

Exercises

Here's an exercise combining the Repel-Impel-Compel and tape recorder techniques. Have a director or friend hit the pause button on your recorder from time to time, unexpectedly. Then, hold that beat (see *On Beats*)—let them rewind and replay it again and again, so that you can explore that beat. Have them stop the tape, and let you improvise. Explore and heighten, just that isolated beat.

Directors can have two new actors go off and tape a scene. They can do it their way, have fun with it. Then the original actors play out the scene to the new recording. Because actors have different tempos, rhythms and feelings, those playing the scene to the other's voices will be forced to listen and change the physical interpretation they had used. In effect, they will manifest physically as another person, which can isolate and reveal the basic principle of acting, i.e. being somebody else. Once grasped, this concept can be applied to every role.

Use the tape technique with monologues, too. Lie on your back in a dark room and listen to the tape while watching yourself as if your mind was a movie screen. See the place in every detail. See how you're dressed in every detail. Is there a window? What's outside? Can you hear anything, smell anything, taste anything, touch anything? As you watch yourself starring here, what movement do you make? Remember, they're called movies because people move in them. Find motivation for moving, i.e., repelled, impelled, compelled.

Do this with scenes, too. If you both see the place alike, that's great. Just refine the details. If not, work it out—you must both be in the same space.

Now retape it again with all these new ideas in your head. Then lie down and watch the movie again, only this time watch yourself in close up the whole time. Move around, get those interesting angles of yours working for you. Be very sensitive to where the light is coming from and how it affects your face. Do not see yourself on stage or in front of a camera—you must see yourself in the actual place.

You will have made giant steps in creating a character. But do not, under *any* circumstance, cling to these choices. They are springboards into further investigation. Never accept your first choice as right—that's lazy (and boring) acting. After explorations and research, it is possible that you may use some of that first choice in your final characterization, but I'll bet my next residual check you won't use it all.

Using the Whelan Tape Technique for Commercial Auditions

Actors say, "I read for a part today", and lots of times it's true. They had their face buried in a script and the casting agent never saw their eyes. Casting people don't care if you can read, they want to see if you can act.

You will usually get at least a few minutes with the copy or script. Find a bathroom or closet and tape it so you can repeat the lines word for word. If you have enough hair to cover the earpiece, they won't even know you're using a tape recorder. They'll think you have a photographic mind.

The casting agents and producers I've shown this technique to like it and find it a big help. The actor is always on camera or able to be seen without having his face looking down at a script. It might sound tricky, but it's really not. You'll feel at ease doing it with just a little practice.

When an Actor Fails to Show Up

I was showcasing my students to a house full of agents, casting agents, directors and producers, and one actor didn't make it to the theater. It seemed his scene partner was out of luck. But then the Whelan tape technique came to the rescue.

I taped the scene with him and substituted for the missing actor. Using the single earpiece, I was able to hear him live and on tape at the same time, and more important, I could hear my own recorded lines and speak simultaneously. With the mini-cassette in my pocket, I was free to relate to him with my eyes and hands. At one point, he slowed down from the way we had taped it. No problem. I slipped my hand into my pocket and hit the pause button. We completed the scene and no one watching knew anything was out of the ordinary.

ON ENVIRONMENT

 behavioral psychologist by the name of Salter once said, "Man is a stomach that got complicated." This refers to stimulus response, meaning that all human activity is a response to some stimulus. For example, for the internal stimulus of hunger, the saliva glands will secrete digestive fluids. For an external stimulus like bright sunlight, you can respond by either seeking shade or sweating. Why is this viewpoint germane to the actor's craft? It has a lot to do with what Viola Spolin calls the *what's beyond*. To me, what's beyond means three environments: immediate, general and external.

Immediate — that which you can reach out and touch or experience without moving.

General — that which you could get to and touch or experience without leaving the place you are in.

External — that which is outside of your space or room. The world you're in, the sounds, colors, images and smells from outside, heard through a wall or seen through a window. The smell of a bakery down the street, a siren, a factory whistle, a church bell, a hunting horn, a car crash. A garden full of roses, a cold breeze that blows through a broken window, a storm raging. Any stimulus that goes on outside and affects the perception of those inside, anything that seeps in from outside and colors your thoughts, words or actions at that very moment.

As you say your line, as you complete your action, how would it be affected by: a gunshot, the shattering of glass, a dance band and the sound of a party, the smell of pizza, the sun setting through a window, a mushroom cloud, a circus passing by, the cops coming to your door, the girl/boy of your dreams walking into the room. How does the outside value add dimension to your performance? Where are you coming from to arrive at the place you are now—a jail? A dance? A dinner? A war? A wedding? A brawl? What happened there, what is still clinging to you from there, as you say that line, perform that action? Where are you going when you leave? What is now on your mind as you say that line, perform that action?

In order to give your performance an immediacy, a verisimilitude, you must relate beyond the skin of your character, out into their *environment!* Details are what move us. That one piece of hair that falls over your eye a certain way that makes you look irresistible or ugly. The broken window, the faded picture of mother, the place where you bought that rug—they're all a part of *the memories for this person*, this character of yours.

Exercise

Start to be more sensitive as to when a specific memory has just entered into your mind and what stimulated that memory. Was it a song? A smell, a picture, a taste, a touch, or a combination of physical stimuli? As soon as you realize that you are lost in memory, race backward and figure out what started it. Did you talk about it and then see the image, or did the image come first? Did you decide not to talk about it? Where did you put the energy it gave you? Was it positive or negative energy? How did it color whatever you were doing or saying at the time it first came into your mind? Think about it right then and there, in your real life!

As you become very conscious of this natural life process, you will then have a firm grasp on the importance of that process being part of your character's *living* on stage.

All the memories:

The body/physical memory
The mental/intellectual memory
The emotional memory

That means your character's dreams, too, for our dreams affect our daily actions and the way we say things. I do not just mean the images you saw the night before while sleeping, but also the dreams of happiness, of revenge, of a world you would like to see. All of your dreams.

Your character is just like anybody else in the world. He has all of these dreams, too. Look at yourself—what are your dreams? How do they affect the things you say and do?

To be in mid-sentence on an important occasion and to have a dream attack with such passion that you stutter or smile "out of nowhere"—*never!* It always comes from somewhere. You may not want to say where that somewhere is, but it was real enough within you to take you over for a time. If this happens to you in life, and it happens to us all, then it must happen to your character, too.

Your character must have a memory—not yours, but something of their own. You must know your character very well. As you're about to see, objects can be a great help in your search for your character's memories.

ON OBJECTS

e all, to some extent, define ourselves by our objects. The clothes we wear, the friends we keep, what things we hold onto, what things we throw away. Look around your room. Pick up or touch five things, objects that are a memory or a souvenir of a place, a person, a time of day. See how strong that memory is. Use the object to stimulate your time travel to the moment that it represents. See how many of the senses you can create from that moment. See, hear, taste, feel, smell that moment.

Now you know how strong an object can be. Realize that your character has those souvenirs, too. Things, objects by which he defines himself. A picture of the Eiffel Tower might represent a dream of the future, a great desire to visit France. A spaceship could be the dream of being an astronaut. There are dreams which pitch us forward and those that push us back.

What five objects are in your character's room? Sometimes, almost always, by figuring out what those objects might be, we get keys or deep insights into our character. Work on your character from all directions.

Look very closely at given circumstance for objects that are part of the character's reality. Orson Welles, in *Citizen Kane,* had one object which defined the motivational and psychological apparatus of his character—"Rosebud," his sled.

Always look for objects in the script, objects that belong to your character. The writer may not even mention the significance of that object; he may indeed not even know why he gave your character that object. It's just a creative flash that stays there on the paper and you as the actor must figure out why. A clue from the Muse—whatever, wherever it came from, it's yours to work with.

If no objects are written into the script, then you must invent them. Does this character have a picture by his bed? Is it Mom, a girl, a child, a dog? On his desk, a coin from a foreign country, a key chain, a statue?

Who knows? You do! It's your part.

Objects—*use them!* They are one of the rare physical tools the actor gets. There are very few in an intangible craft. Seize on them and the life-giving quality they have for your character.

If some of your character's dreams and memories overlap with yours, use your own objects. If they give the right feeling at the right time, you relate to them easier as long as you can get back to your character in time and style for the next beat.

Before your first line of dialogue, contact an object that has emotional significance to the scene. See it, see the place as it would be in real life—

colors, sounds, smells. Objects can help you define your character.

Everything you read or learn has an application to acting, for everything is about people or the world they live in.

A trace is but a chain of nerve cells linked by "synapses" where a nerve impulse jumps from one cell to the next. These connections are vital to trace formation, so researchers led by William Greenough of the University of Illinois decided to see how synapses change when memories form. They raised some rats in cages filled with toys and others in nearly empty cages. Their finding: rats in the complex environment grew 20 percent more synapses in part of their cortex than the deprived rats did. Perhaps synapses, which form as the rats process information about the props in the cage, are the seeds of memories.

Reprinted with permission from Newsweek, September 29th, 1986

Props help memory—use them in rehearsals. Look for them in the script—if they're in the script they are given circumstance. If not, invent them.

I had an actor in my workshop in Hollywood that resisted object work. For weeks he kept saying, "This is stupid—why are we doing this?" I wanted to kill him.

One day he came in and as the class started to settle in for work, he asked to say something. He told us all about an audition for a major TV episode he had the day before. The part was a cop, and even though no gun was written into the script he decided to invent one, miming the cleaning of his gun while doing his lines. The casting agent was intrigued by the skillful way he handled the "weapon" and he got the part.

That is a $5,000 to $10,000 lesson, as he could earn that amount, depending on residuals. (I thought about charging him a percentage, but I figured his confession to the class was payment enough).

> *"I used to act for fun.*
> *Now I act for money,*
> *and it's even more fun!"*

ON ACTING FOR FILM, T.V. AND COMMERCIALS

cting is acting, and that is true. However, there are technical differences between working on stage and working before a camera. Here's a quick list.

1. **Closeups** – Most important is that you must be able to do a powerful two person scene *by yourself.* The reason is that in closeup you're the only person in the picture. And let's say the other person that you've been working with has gone home for the day or is already doing another movie in some other country. And now reading their lines is the producer's nephew off camera.

    This will happen to you. But remember, it's *your closeup* and that's what you take to the bank. You'd better be able to do it.

    For exercise, say you're working on a scene with a partner and you've got it nailed. The next time you do it as a camera closeup, have some non-actor stand behind a bright light so you can't see them and read your partner's lines totally flat. See if you can maintain energy, enthusiasm, the power of your performance.

Love scenes are great for this. Instead of the beautiful girl you're doing the scene with, have some production assistant-type stand there so *you can see them* and let them read your partner's lines in their own uninspired way— flat. See if you can keep the high level of performance you've had.

2. **Matching** – In films, TV and commercials, you shoot out of sequence. You might start a shoot one day and finish it hours or days later. You have to remember exactly what you were wearing. Was the cigarette just lit, half smoked or what? Was the glass in your right hand or was it the left? On major productions, there will be a continuity person to help keep track of all this, and they are very sharp. But even if they don't get every little detail, *the editor will* and you can lose the best closeup of your life because your collar was up in the master shot and the next day or after lunch when you shot the closeup, it was down. Polaroids are used a lot, but it's nobody's closeup but yours. So mind what you do and how you do it.

3. **Looping and Dubbing** – At some point, you will have to loop or dub sound. For some reason, the sound track is no good. (In film, as a rule, sound is done separately from the picture and is married to it later). So now you have to go back and do it again. *Dubbing* means that you add your voice but you're not seen on camera, or your

back is to the camera. *Looping* means that you must record your lines while matching the movement of your lips on the screen. It's called looping because a small section of film is cut out and shown over and over and over again until the lines you're recording are perfectly in sync.

Now the major problem here is not the sync but the quality of your voice. Once I had to go back and lay in some dialog on a feature *six months later.*

I had to match a voice I had used—a dialect, a style—that I woke up with one morning in Florida. I'm sure you've noticed that your voice changes even during the day. So it can be tough to get this right months later.

There's no camera, no sets, no costume, nothing in the recording studio to recreate that high energy you had while shooting. You must work very hard to recreate your character. There are a lot of technical demands and you can get caught up. *Hold on to your character.* Start with the highest, most emotional lines. The recording studio's pretty sterile, and this will get your blood running and help snap you back into character. So start with those super-charged lines, even if you have to go back and redo them at the tail of the session.

4. **Where's Your Look?** – If you're doing a scene or closeup and you have to relate (that is, see a

person or event that is off camera)—ask, "Where's my look?" *Be very specific.* Always go to the same spot. If it's a person, make sure they are always at the exact same height.

If they tell you your look is "over there," then find something to focus on. A crack in the wall, a tree with a knot on it. Be very specific. Focus on something.

5. **Types of Shots** – Always ask, "Where's my frame?" A long shot (L.S.) means your *whole body will be in frame.* A medium shot (M.S.) means part of your body will be in frame, usually the upper torso. A closeup (C.U.) means your neck and head will be in frame. An extreme closeup (E.C.U.) could be just your face or eyes or left nostril.

    Now the reason you've got to know this is obvious. You can't bounce around in a closeup or you'll bounce right out of frame. But another good reason is that you shouldn't waste energy on some part of the body that will not be seen.

    Years ago, a friend of mine who was a very talented actor took me to the set of a series he was starring in. He had asked for his frame and was told it would be a closeup. He walked over to me and said, "Watch me real closely on this one." What I saw really blew me away. I watched all the energy leave every other part of his body and travel up to his face. I mean, I watched it go from his toes back through his feet, up his legs and chest, and up into his face.

Don't waste energy on parts of the body that are not in the frame.

6. **Delivering on Time** – In film, but especially in commercials, time is super important. You have to find the dramatic truth by doing the lines the way you feel them while rehearsing. Then, if it takes 30 seconds, be ready to do it in five. The producer will be standing there with a stop watch (I'm serious). You have got to find that one word that you can draw out—accent—and rip through the rest.

7. **Hitting a Mark** – To get a picture just the way he or she wants it, your director will want you to be in an exact spot when you say a line. That spot is called a *mark*. This is usually just a piece of tape on the floor of the studio. Outside, it might be a line drawn in the sand with your foot.

The problem is that you can never look at your mark. You have to feel it in your bones. The easiest way is to count your steps. You can mark off a piece of furniture or some other stationary object. I don't like to mark off other actors because they might not be as consistent or as careful as I am.

If you want to know how close you've got to be to your mark, you'll get the idea when the assistant camera person pulls the tape measure from the camera lens to the edge of your eye.

It takes practice and experience, but you'll get it. Take it seriously. Know your *first position* (that is, where you start from—you'll hear it a lot: "First positions, everyone.")

While the rest of the shot is being set up, instead of chit-chatting with some actor or technical person, count your steps from your first position to your mark, over and over until you're hitting it perfectly. Do it until it feels natural and you can say your lines without worrying about it.

As an exercise, put a piece of tape on your floor and practice hitting it with your eyes closed. Sometimes you have two or three marks to hit in a single scene.

8. **Concentration in Film** – If you've worked on stage, you've been a little spoiled. You're working in continuity. You've another actor to work off of. You're in character for a long time. The house is dark and the audience is quiet (hopefully). All this is conducive to sustaining concentration.

A film set or location can be like acting in the middle of a freeway. Grips pounding nails. Gaffers hanging huge lights overhead. Camera people, makeup and sound people running everywhere. Then somebody yells, "Quiet on the set" and it all freezes. You do two minutes of acting, the director yells "Cut," and all hell breaks loose again. If it's an M.O.S. shot (literally, M.O.S. means "mit out sound" from an old Hollywood story of a German director referring to a scene shot without sound), the director might be talking you through the scene: "O.K., now kiss her neck." So you might have to keep your concentration for a shorter time than on stage. But you've got to get there a lot quicker. And go in a lot deeper just to hold on to it. A tip: learn to play chess. It strengthens concentration.

9. **Don't Jump the Gun** – Wait for *"Action!"* to start a scene. The director is the only one who can say "Action!"

   And never, ever stop acting until you hear, "Cut!" The director is the only one who can say "Cut!"

   If you blow a line, you might want to stop. But the director might love what you've been doing up to that point and might want to see where it will go from there. Maybe he wants to see how you use the frustration of blowing a line. He may like the reaction of the other actor in the scene. He may be a sick man. But until he says *"Cut!"* you keep on acting, because that's your job.

   The major difference between acting for the stage and film is that on stage you rehearse, you have previews, and your character continues to grow with every performance. In film you must have a complete, polished character from day one of shooting—sometimes you shoot the last part of a film first. That character has to be all there. So your rehearsal period must be much more intense.

I'm starting an eight week shoot on a film tomorrow. My character will grow in the eight weeks, but the discoveries must be very subtly integrated.

ON AUDITIONS

hen you work on stage, you work big. It's a much broader approach to a character. You use the whole body, and the facial movements are bigger, too.

I believe that when you rehearse, you can get into character faster by rehearsing for the stage, even if you are to do your performance for the camera.

There's a principle here that also applies to audition situations.

Now take this with a grain of salt—you must be sensitive to the audition environment. If you're doing a play in a one hundred seat house, your moves are smaller than in a one thousand seat house. But what I'm saying is to *be big in auditions*.

I, and all the other directors I know, would always prefer to tell an actor to internalize or, "Pull it back some." This means keep what you've got— the energy, etc.—but just put it inside of you. Directors would much rather do that than say, "Could you give me a little more energy?" A director shouldn't have to beg.

I can create anything out of energy, but I cannot create energy. That non-energetic actor is out. So go a little big in auditions. 95% of the time, you'll be better off for that choice.

Looking for an Audition Piece

I tell my students that the hardest thing they will have to do in my class will be to find the right audition piece. Some tips:

A) The camera doesn't lie. If you're 20 years old, find a part for a 20 year old.

A girl was auditioning for my class, and she was 17 and looked it. She started to set up the scene for me and something sounded wrong. I asked her how old her character was, and she replied 40 years.

"Sit down," I said. "You might do that in high school, you might even do it in college. But you will never do that in Hollywood. You're a pretty young girl."

She asked if she should just do pretty young girl parts. "Yes," I replied. But think about it. In her age range, she has lots of room to express herself, to use her talent. How many kinds of 17 year old girls are there in this world? There are:

- 17 year old junkie street sluts
- 17 year old Princesses
- 17 year old New England preppies
- 17 year old valley girls
- 17 year old sophisticated girls (17 going on 30)
- 17 year old illiterate backwoods girls

And so on, and so on.

If you're 17, *you're not going to get cast in a movie, TV show or a commercial as a 30 year old.* Get real! Do you want to work, or don't you? Find a piece in which people would believe your age if your face were blown up on a movie screen to 60 feet by 40 feet.

B) Pick a piece written within the last five years. None of my students can do work more than five years old (we do some Shakespeare early in the class, but that's so I can see what I've got to work with). New material has the advantage of not colliding in a casting director's head with the 8000 other actors he has seen doing the same part. I feel like if I see one more "Eddie & May" (from Sam Shepard's *Fool For Love*), I will go to sleep. If you've got strong, fresh material then they are really watching *you*.

C) Pick a piece that will win you an Oscar, make you a star. Find one where you start out crying and wind up laughing, or start out loving and wind up hating—a broad range of life or death in three minutes, max. Don't do quiet, talking, sitting scenes. *Go big!* Knock them on their butts with your power and your broad emotional range and do it in three minutes, max.

D) Most audition scenes are taken from plays. Now think about this: the writer has two hours or so in the course of his play to make his point, but you as an actor in an audition situation have only three minutes. In a short play the writer has only one third to one half the time to make his point. So the writer is going to tighten up his material a lot, doubling your chances of finding a good audition piece. But even in a short play a writer will have an hour to make the hot scenes happen. So when you find a hot scene, change it, tighten it even more. If you've been rehearsing properly—taking chances, improvising—you may discover a twist, a hook, a joke, whatever, that makes it better than it was before. So change it! All you have to do is preface your scene with "adapted from" such and such a play by so and so.

My apologies to writers who go up in flames after reading this (I am also one of you). I am speaking as an actor to actors, and our problems are different from yours.

So—use short plays, and chop them up if you need to.

E) Many plays have stage directions, such as (sits down) or (starts crying) or (not looking at her). Mostly, you can cross this stuff out as soon as you see it and forget it.

These are acting editions, and these directions are from some other director to some other actor sometime in the past. It's your part now. You may want to laugh where the thing says (cries). Do it your way!

Of course, use your head with this. Some of those directions are given circumstance. If it says (slaps her), and her next line is, "Why did you slap me?", ok. But mostly, this stuff is junk.

F) It's fairly easy to go through books of selected scenes which have been compiled for actors, find one you like and then get the whole play. But because this is the easy way, the material is usually overexposed.

G) It may mean hours of searching in the library or elsewhere, but once you've found the right piece, you can use it for a few years. In the library, the sources you should use are:

1. New York theater critic's reviews
2. Film Review Annual
3. Best Plays
4. Best Short Plays
5. Best One Act Plays

All of these have reviews, synopses and commentary. Besides helping you sort through a ton of material in a hurry, they help you know what's going on in theatre and film today.

Notice what things are said about actors and performances, faults and graces, what is admired and what is disliked. You can then be sensitive to these in your own work, and hopefully eliminate the faults.

Reviews will also help you to know names of actors, directors and producers. This is the Who's Who of your world—who's doing the kind of work you'd like to do, and where to find them.

So *read reviews.*

As a final note in this section, check out the movies and plays being cast right now. If a character description fits you perfectly, submit yourself by mail or go to the audition. Each of you is right for some part right now. The odds may be one in 1000, but you are right for it. As you study and improve your talent, the odds may become five in 1000, and they will continue to improve.

Finding a strong audition piece will help you a great deal.

ON OBJECTIVES

The overriding reason anyone is with anyone else on stage or in life is that they want something from that other person — love, sex, money, whatever. That's what actors call an objective.

You must know what you want. Then you can work on the sensory, physical, emotional and intellectual tools you will need to get it. To know it means to put it into words as well as to sense its meaning.

The idea is that a musician does not attempt to learn a whole symphony all at once. He breaks it down into movements, sections, progressions, measures, bars, beats. Actors do this, too. The outline of our work is the script.

A super objective is what your character wants overall. An objective is what he wants right now. For example, say your character's super objective is to build a great railroad, but he looks up while tying his shoe to see a train coming, so his objective becomes to get the hell out of the way.

A few more examples of objectives:

To win friendship

To make a buck

To do a job

To get her home

To fight back

To have fun

You get the idea. Now you can structure the emotional variations (subtle shades of feeling learned from your emotional expansion exercises with your thesaurus and dictionary) necessary to achieve your objective in the most interesting way.

An important note: I have been talking about completed objectives — this does not mean an achieved objective. An objective can be achieved or thwarted; a failed objective supplies the impetus for the next objective in the same way an achieved objective does. How do you act when you do not get what you want? How do you act when you do? They both show you the transition which is the key to the next objective.

ON BEATS

ou always hear actors and directors talking about beats and there is sometimes confusion as to what a beat really is. The term is used two ways.

In usage "A", it is like a musical beat or snapping your fingers to a tune. A director might say, "Take two beats, then come through the door."

In usage "B", a beat is an emotion. Acting is going from emotion to emotion in a theatrical manner, not as you would, but as your character would.

All you have to do is experience one honest emotion/beat from the depths of your character and you're half way home. You will probably discover the "tip" of that emotion the first time you do the Whelan Tape Technique. You should get a very strong Repel-Impel-Compel (RIC), if not the first time, the second or third time for sure.

Beats—A very simple, exaggerated example:

(Beat: *Joyous anticipation*) **Phil**
(He enters apartment down left, with a small package in one hand behind his back. He smiles at Rita.) "Hi!"

(Beat: *Very angry*)   **Rita**

"You bastard, don't smile at me. I have been waiting three hours. I was worried sick about you, then Mary called. She said she saw you in the jewelry story with your secretary. Get out! I never want to see you again!"

(Beat: *Hurt*)   **Phil**

(Moving to her, holding out the package) "I was not running around buying jewelry for my secretary. I was getting this for you. Julie just happened to come in the shop—she was getting her watch fixed! We chatted while I waited for this."

(Beat: *Deeply embarrassed*)**Rita**

(Opens the box and sees a diamond wedding ring) "Oh! It's beautiful! I feel like a complete ass!" (She looks at the ring and tears show in her eye).

(Beat: *Forgiving*)   **Phil**

(Taking her in his arms, lifting her face so they are looking in each other's eyes.) "I like a jealous woman." (He leans into her. They kiss).

(Beat: *Joy*)   **Rita**

(Smiles warmly) "How did I ever get so lucky?"

So, in these few lines, the actress playing Rita has three beats:

1. Jealous anger
2. Deep embarrassment
3. Joy

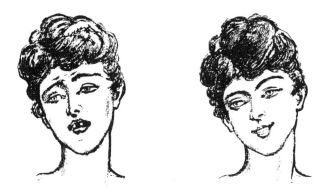

***Acting is going from emotion to emotion
as your character would***

Now take out your thesaurus and look up
jealousy and anger. Make a list in order of growing
intensity for each. Are there any words there that
you did not expect to find?

In my last role, my character was very jealous
and I was playing it sincere, but it was a cliché. So I
got out my thesaurus and looked up jealousy, and
beneath the common words I found "concern."
Thinking about that word took me out of the hot-
headed, Latin approach I'd been using. My
reasoning was if you're jealous, it is because you feel
you're losing. But instead of the "hammer-on and
demand" approach, you might try being extra
considerate, extra loving.

I tried this, and in places it worked superbly. It
gave the scenes and my character extra variety,
extra interest.

The thesaurus technique will give every role you do more colors. If you get one more it might be the winning color. How many games are won by one point—one run—one goal. Those games are big business, too—look at athletes' salaries. Then look at actors' salaries, and figure one extra color is something you should be willing to work for.

ON IMAGINATION

ctors must be able to adopt any set of beliefs from which human beings function. In other words, they must be flexible.

Acting is more than a job, it is a way of life. It is a philosophy which is ever changing. It must be fluid and eclectic to keep up with all aspects of the "Human Condition."

This is not to say you cannot have deep feelings as to the proper course of conduct in life. It merely means you must be able to be a Catholic one day, a Jew the next and a Satanist the next. A Freudian on Monday, a Behaviorist on Tuesday.

Each and all of these attitudes are structures by which various characters (people) pattern their lives. They are, therefore, *clues* (given circumstances) either from the author of the script or your creative imagination. These clues to human behavior will have a profound influence on your character's choices, thought patterns and modes of expression.

You must be able to imagine these states of existence. Put muscles in your imagination. Work it and work it hard, building bridges to the audience's imagination. Exercise imagination with the intensity of a body builder. What happens to them on the outside will happen to you on the inside.

A body builder and an artist are equally diligent in their daily work habits. You must exercise your imagination every day. You must imagine that you are someone else, with someone else's faults and problems. Think how they think, eat what they eat, wear what they wear, go to their church, their jail. You *must* do this when you get a part, but you cannot wait for a big part to do it. A baseball player does not wait until he gets to the "Big League" to learn how to swing a bat. He is taught and then he trains and is coached. He works to improve his ability. He does exercises to build the muscles he will need to be better and stronger.

You must train your imagination that way.

Imagination is the water of our creative lives, concentration the food. How does the imagination of the artist differ from the imagination of the ordinary person? First of all, the artist must strip his mind of any prejudice, and I do mean *all* prejudice, of good as well as evil. Conventional morality is exactly that, a morality for those who lead conventional lives. Quite often, this means people without a morality of their own. So they adopt one by convention. The artist must transcend that limited view of the universe and see himself as the center, a piece of the sun from whom emanates new ideas, concepts, and ultimately modes of expression.

You might get a part which has you being a hatchet murderer who totally enjoys his work. Conventional morality would forbid the imagination from speculating with pure glee about chopping up dear old Mother. However, as a actor, that is exactly what you must do. It is your job.

If a pure, innocent girl gets the part of a hardened prostitute, conventional morality would prohibit her from dwelling for long periods on the sexual activity that is the bread and butter of the prostitute's life. We, as actors, must have the courage to penetrate into the darkest and brightest areas of the human condition, to dwell there without fear or pain. When the part is done, it is done and now we can look for our next one.

What about the poor atheist who gets the part of a priest? His personal beliefs must be put aside. He must read the Bible and go to church. He must defend, to him, the defenseless—championing causes which, for him, normally are a source of contempt. Personal prejudice must be dissolved if artistic truth is to be achieved.

Exercises

Go to a movie that you would never go to. Read a book that you would never read. Watch a TV show that you would never watch. Buy a magazine that you would never buy and read it all. Talk to someone you would never talk to, listening a lot, drawing them out. What do they like or dislike? What do they eat, or not eat? What do they think about the government, religion, sex? Always ask yourself why they feel the way they do. Find out about their backgrounds. Watch their physical traits, habits, nervous ticks. Observe how they eat, smoke and drink.

Imagine for a day that you are God. Look around the world at what you would change, realizing that people have free wills. You cannot snap your fingers and change that. How can you influence things and make them go your way? Make a list. Spend a few hours on it.

Imagine you are the Devil. You cannot snap your fingers and change people's free will, either. How would you make things go your way? Spend the same amount of time making a list.

Imagine there is no God and no Devil. What would you change? And how? Imagine you are:

The President of the U.S.A.
Six years old
The Mayor of Philadelphia
Ghandi
Christ
Hitler
Napoleon
A tiger
A snake
A seagull
A rapist
A Democrat
An air-head
A lawyer
A cab driver

What do they all have in common? What makes them different?

Imagine, always, everywhere. Be a dreamer. Be the Arnold Schwarzenegger of imagination. Imagination is a muscle. Exercise it. Avoid atrophy. It's fun, and you'll be a more interesting person (actor), too.

ON STAGE RELATIONSHIPS and CHARACTER DEVELOPMENT

uman beings don't like to be called animals but that's what we are. What I'm saying here is to have an animal awareness of whomever else is on stage with you—*see* them, *smell* them, *touch* them, *hear* them and *taste* them. The best performance is one in which we see someone really *feel* something.

Relationships Through The Senses

If it's hot, it's hot. If it's a glass, it's a glass. Feel it, touch it, smell whatever is in it. If it's supposed to be whiskey and it's really iced tea, so what. If you really smell that iced tea, the audience will see someone who is really smelling something and it will be a truthful action. Your sense will be operating and that is the important thing—a real human being really smelling something.

If you touch someone, *touch them.* Whoever you're touching, really touch them, feel them. What's it like—their skin temperature. Feel it through the tips of your fingers, your lips. Experience that sensation, totally, completely; wet, dry, the exact temperature of lips in a kiss. Feel, with your back, a subway crowd. With your front, a dance, a hug. Feel that *character.* How do you feel about him, not the actor, but the person, the character opposite you? Just see them as that person, that character. It is a warm body that answers you, talks to you, looks at you, does things with you, and you do things back. *It is called acting.*

Feel your relationship to that other body by heat. Concentrate, never lose consciousness of their proximity by smell. Listen to how they are walking, how they are breathing. Otherwise, you're talking to yourself, and you can't hear anything, either.

If you're supposed to kiss a girl, forget that she's not your girlfriend, wife or old flame. *Kiss* that girl—kiss her so well that she follows you home after the show. There's no obligation—it's a professional situation. But enjoy it—most actresses are fun to kiss. It's one of the perks that go with a

Kiss her so well she follows you home after the show

tough job. (Of course, this applies to girls kissing guys, too.) Gene Hackman said, "Acting is strange. You fly in to do a film, walk onto a set and get introduced to a girl, then 15 minutes later you're in bed with her!"

It sounds easy, but try it with 50 people running around on the set, someone powdering your nose, a director whispering in your ear, hot lights in your eyes and cameras rolling.

It applies to all the senses—*be an animal up there.*

If you're supposed to be eating or drinking something good, make it clear to "Props" to make something good, so that you can get an honest response out of it. You can't always do this— sometimes you have to do it the hard technical way. But whenever you can, make it easy on yourself.

Relationships Through a Group

Everybody's a groupie—an economic groupie, social groupie, athletic groupie, religious groupie. Groups are groups because they have *something in common.* As actors, our concern is what group or groups do our characters belong to and how does that affect their physical expression. This is not just for groups like handicapped vets—imagine an aristocratic tea that the Hell's Angels were mistakenly invited to. The manners of a group will show as a physical manifestation of a member of that group. As a member of a group, your character will somehow conform to that group.

Plays and movies are written about groups confronted by individuals: breaking into a group (the new kid in town), breaking out of a group (leaving your family), moving up in a group (an ambitious politician), moving down in a group (a washed up athlete).

To know your character, you need to know his or her group. How does that group act? How do they talk? Check their usage of the English language, with regional dialects or special slang.

What sort of aspirations does this group have? There are small groups and large groups, football players, miners, nuns, salesgirls, executives, Indians, Russians, Poles. What is their percentage of divorces, suicides? What is the stress factor for your character's group?

There are plenty of facts on groups in books. You can find them—this is your homework. Build memory banks for them. *Character: everything flows from it.*

Relationships Through Memory

What we are doing with all these tasks is to distract ourselves away from the consciousness of acting. We are building that cross current of thoughts, feelings, sensations that distract us all as human beings. We are building the years of memories that go to make up a human being, those memories which are always moving in and out, over, under, and beside the conscious act we are trying to perform at the moment.

Whether you are making dinner, getting a driver's license or climbing stairs, you can be suddenly stopped by a thought, a simple action interrupted by *memory*—physical, intellectual or emotional memories. These things happen all the time to people, but not to an actor waiting for a cue, intent on playing a role. You have to feel, think, do something if that character is going to be alive up there. Something real has to complement or obstruct what is being done by the actor.

There are ten billion neurons in the brain:

200,000 for temperature,
500,000 for touch,
3,000,000 for pain,
billions for interpreting the sensory input of the
    moment,
billions for memory,
billions for dreams.

How you gonna match that?

I'll tell you how. Hard work, doing everything you've been taught to do. Given circumstance, use of objects, biography of character, finding objectives/ beats, and all the exercises in concentration and character exploration that you've been taught and will be taught. In other words, do your job as an actor. Do your homework (by yourself), and your rehearsals (with your partners and director). Then, when the curtain goes up, step right out there and do it. Do your best, and trust the creativity in you that made you want to be an actor in the first place. When you feel you've earned the right, being that person is almost easy.

Building Physical Memory

Two guys in a class in L.A. were doing a cop scene. It was good acting, but something wasn't clicking. Although it wasn't part of the scene, I told them to clean their weapons as they did the lines. It soon became obvious that neither one had ever handled a gun. But cops carry guns all day, every day, on and off duty. They practice with them, clean them, collect them. The guns are a part of their lives— *their lives depend on them.* These two guys were supposed to be hardcore, veteran cops, but they were fumbling with their guns. So I talked to them, and they both admitted that they hated guns.

I told them that it was OK to be a cop that hates guns, but you still have to carry one. You have to know how to use it, and you will use it to protect your life or your partner's life. I told them to go out to a firing range and do some shooting before they did the scene again.

The next time they did the scene it was much more exciting. They now had some *physical memory* in their muscles, in their skin and bones. They had felt the cold touch of the metal, the recoil of a gun firing, experienced the hand-eye coordination of pointing a gun at a target, heard the explosion of a gun firing, and tasted the acid smell of burnt gunpowder in the air.

Building Intellectual Memory

I'm doing a part right now of a Romanian count, an ambassador to France at the start of World War II, who is living in Washington.

I've been reading books on the education of young nobles, books on diplomacy and the diplomatic corps at that time, books on Romania and books on Nazis. I've been listening to Romanian music and Nazi music. I am, in short, using any source I possibly can to find out everything about this person and his time. I am building his *intellectual memory*.

I even found a Romanian who had been living here a short time, and I invited him and his wife to a rehearsal. Afterwards I took them home to tea and asked a ton of questions, and taped him reading a few long monologues to use as accent guides.

I work on parts until they are done, until the play is over. During the run, when I had stretches back stage, I read a 600 page biography of Queen Marie of Romania. I was constantly building my character's memories.

Building Emotional Memory

This is the hardest part. This is where acting becomes art.

Through script analysis, given circumstance, beat analysis and objectives, we see what broad emotions must be played, *felt*. Then (recalling the chapter on emotions) we drag out our thesaurus and break the emotions into many colors. Now, because we have some physical and intellectual memories in place, we stir them all up to see what comes out.

It's tough—you have to use yourself in some ways. But you have to do more or you'll just be playing yourself. Most often, films and plays will have you doing most of your heavy emotional stuff with one other person—a wife, a lover, a partner.

Recently, I made a video in L.A. I had three characters who were Vietnam vets—they had saved each other's lives, partied hard together, loved each other. The three actors I cast had never met each other when they showed up for their first rehearsal. There was a strip joint called the Kit-Kat Club across the street from the theatre where we were working. When they came in, scripts in hand and sizing each other up, I took twenty dollars out of the budget and told them to go across the street, shoot some pool, flirt with some girls and have a great time. I didn't want to see them again until our next rehearsal, five o'clock the next day. They got the idea, and in the end did a great job for me.

Years later, I'm still running into these actors, and they tell me that so-and-so's in New York doing a show with Joe Papp or something. They are still friends after that one afternoon.

On another occasion, I was directing a film in L.A., and my leads were to be lovers. Both were attractive, interesting people. They showed up for a first rehearsal and I told them that I was going to be busy for a few hours. Since it was a beautiful day, I suggested they go to a large park and have a picnic—wine and cheese and fruit and such (again, I hit the budget). I called the male lead aside and told him to play his guitar, pour wine for her, be romantic and try to seduce her—but be back in two hours. I then called his opposite over and said, "I just told him to try to seduce you. I don't really care what happens, but play along, enjoy the game, make him think that there's a chance—but make him work for it."

That also worked out very well. What I'm saying is get to know who you are working with, if at all possible. If you are supposed to be friends with a character, try to be friends with the actor.

If it is impossible, then it is impossible. But there is a story in Hollywood: an actor asks, "What's my motivation?" and the director replies, "Your paycheck—now get out there and do it!"

Exercises

In workshops, these three exercises have really helped students achieve total involvement with character.

1. *The Finger Snap Technique*— After an actor has delivered a speech, his scene partner can not respond until the director snaps his or her fingers. The actor must concentrate on what has just been said and how it makes him feel. Each actor must stay in the scene and stay in character no matter how long it takes. When the director sees the actor has really connected with the emotion, a snap of the fingers lets the scene proceed.

One useful side effect of this exercise is that actors are forced to really explore the place and objects in the scene. A lot of useable stage business comes from this.

So how can you apply this idea to your private rehearsals? Simply by agreeing with your scene partner to sometimes take time to explore the emotions in your lines. If you want to take five or even fifteen minutes to connect to a particular emotion, you will—and you will not speak until you are honestly connected. Stick with it for as long as it takes. This exercise usually comes after all lines have been learned.

2. *Talking Out Your Inner Monologue* — In this exercise, you say out loud what your character is saying silently to himself. Use an accent when you speak with this inner voice. For example:

Karen

(in say a German accent) "Here comes that guy who wants to work for my dad. If he's nice, maybe I'll put in a good word for him."

(then in her normal voice) "Hi, Bob. Are you headed in to see my father today? I know he's expecting you. By the way, do you like my new dress?"

Bob

(in perhaps an Irish accent) "God, I don't want to hurt her feelings, but she looks like a houseboat in that thing! But if I tell her that, I'll never get that job."

(then in his normal voice) "Hey, very colorful! You look great in red!"

You get the idea. Before you speak, say everything that comes to mind regarding what's just been said to you. This can take a lot of time, but it's worth it.

It's best to do this as you rehearse, but if you're someone who has trouble thinking on your feet, write this inner monologue out instead.

Personally, I also write out where my character is and what he's doing when not on camera or on stage, complete with place descriptions and dialogue if he's with other people.

3. *Seeing Pictures* — If your character is talking about the Grand Canyon, make sure you have a picture of the Grand Canyon in your head. If you're talking about someone you met and it was pleasant, see that meeting in full detail — their clothes, the sound of their voice, the color of their eyes, everything.

Look for images in your lines. Create a series of images for your role, like your own private slide show inside your head. It will help bring more life and richness to your performance.

ON SOUND

ften, you can find sounds that when tape recorded will stimulate your creativity, whether they are directly related to the scene you are doing or not.

Related Example: For a beach house scene, tape the waves crashing and the gulls squawking. Let it play as you perform the whole scene, realizing that sound is everywhere, and scenes are not conducted in a vacuum.

In a movie, this sound effect may be added later, but your private rehearsals will be much more effective with sound. Later, even though you are on an absolutely silent sound stage, your actor's instrument will have those sounds programmed in and your performance will be richer for it.

Unrelated Example: If the scene is an argument, a tape of a prize fight could work. Or, you could play a song which somehow puts you in that mood. Almost all libraries have sound effects records.

ON GIBBERISH

Using gibberish on first reading of lines is like translating to a foreign language. How does the line feel? What is its rhythm? Where are the pauses? What is its volume range? Does it go up-down, down-up, from a whisper to a shout, or stay all one level?

Take immediate emotional control of the line. Take instant access to the life, the *subtext* of the line without the need to juggle the symbols created by words and their meaning. The concrete words block the intuitive emotions, and quite often they do not mean what they say—perhaps the total opposite. Through gibberish, you will discover what they mean emotionally, and then you can say them with the correct sensitivity.

Words and feelings are natural, whether the feelings are conveyed by the words or are opposite to the words. They are organically fused by the spontaneity of life.

In acting, *words are the frozen essence of the thoughts and feelings which prompted them.* You cannot overlay them with emotion. You must discover that emotion by penetrating into the word.

Give your intuition a chance. Use gibberish at the first reading, and at many subsequent rehearsals, explore the feelings and sensations that will be there when you do gibberish. Now the words will have proper tempo, volume, speed and emotion.

Gibberish is one of the most valuable techniques you will ever learn. Use it in every part you do. Practice it as you would French or Spanish. Expand your facility with it.

It is an express train to the emotional meaning of the words you use. And, more importantly, to the words you don't use. It illuminates the between-the-lines meaning of what you are saying faster, quicker, better than any other technique you will ever learn.

So, OK—what is it? That is the hard part. For what it is, is a non-language language. It is not double talk, it is not pig latin. It is closer to a jazz scat: scooby doobie wah wah wah.

It is syllables and consonants all mixed up. Maybe it is what Armenian sounds like to you if you are not Armenian. It is what your electric typewriter or word processor looks like when it goes nuts. "Olag nes leosh! Ealk wen ein tojie tow ollo, keit is wog wi hie waw tha quoth gark. Oth idi hou woh otho quix?"

Say that like you were asking for a bus pass, or ordering a meal in a restaurant and you have the idea. Notice that all "words" are distinctly pronounceable.

Make up your own words for every line in your script. Don't write them down, just let them come out of your mouth as you move through your part.

Don't remember them.

If your character wants a drink from his wife—

John

"Distog perliep na!"

Mary

"Nagak druzog of ata."

Make up new ones all the time. It's your language. You will very quickly see that being free of the words puts you on a direct line with the emotion meant to be communicated or hidden by the lines. Explore, experiment. Allow the emotion to come through. Go for it! This is one of the best techniques—*acting is communicating changing emotions.*

Watch foreign language films. You will see you know much of what is happening by the looks, postures and gestures of the actors.

With gibberish, you will soon notice that you are acting with your whole body. You look harder at your partner, you are concentrating much better. You are more involved with the objects and the other actors in the scene.

Gibberish is not direct translation, line by line. It is simply sensing the emotion your character is feeling and expressing it in a non-language verbal pattern.

Don't translate word for word, or you kill it. Let it fall out of your mouth. Just get to the emotion in the lines and let it gerlap dorilk absco pepac flam.

ON REHEARSAL PROCEDURE FOR STUDENT ACTORS

n rehearsing scenes for workshop, there must be a creative interplay. It will sometimes happen that one actor has more experience, more ability. Feeling superior, he will try to take over the scene. He will try to force his idea of exactly how it should be done on the other actor. Not only is this not positive, it is absolutely destructive. In negating your partner's choices, in failing to respect his creativity, in not listening or caring about what the other element in your scene feels, you are setting up an antagonism. This antagonism will run deep, even if he does acquiesce.

Think about the actor who has been stomped on in this manner. There will always be an element of doubt in his mind about his choices, as well as resentment over having been denied his creative input. That is why, in the professional world, *no actor is ever permitted to comment on another actor's performance*. That is why you have a director. If you are having problems with another actor, you go to the director and explain. Then let him handle it. In workshop situations you have a director as well, and if a problem of interpretation arises, you take it to him. That is his job. That is one of the prime reasons he is there. Be professional.

Say you are in a show with a star (and this can happen) and the star is way off the mark and not giving you a chance. He might be telling you how to do your part, or he might not be doing his part the way you truly believe he must in order to get the sense of the scene across. If you tell the star his business, you will in most cases be *fired*. The star has more weight, and is more important to the success of the piece than you are. If he does not want you around, you get fired.

If you had been professional, you would have gone to the director and talked it over with him. He may find the compromise that will satisfy all parties concerned.

In workshop, you may by necessity be directing yourselves at first. You must respect each other's creativity, and listen to each other. Discover betwee₁ you the meaning, intent and mode of expres;ion for the scene. If it turns out that you and your partner have totally opposite ideas about the scene, try it both ways then meet with your director and get his input on the work.

ON THE DEMAND
FOR REHEARSAL

here are three types of memory:
Physical memory
Intellectual memory
Emotional memory
Integrating these is only possible through rehearsal. The French call this "repetition," but it is not simple repetition. It is creative exploration to discover the most dramatic physical manifestation of the series of emotional changes (beats) which go to make up your character. The writer wrote the words, but it's up to you to add the movement and lyricism, to see the pictures. You build each of the three memories, more or less separately. Integration of these memories comes only through rehearsal.

You build each memory, the physical memory, the intellectual memory and the emotional memory, either brick by brick or with explosive creative leaps. The latter process you simply obey. With the former, you must inspect each brick of each memory, throwing away chipped and cracked material. It's a tough job, acting, and I am not apologizing for the fact that there must be *rehearsal!*

Break that word into syllables—Re•hears•al. To re-hear all.

This is where all discoveries are made during the beginning stages of the work on a role, and later where all your finishing touches are polished. It is where the foundation of your character is built.

Get the point! Start wrong for lack of rehearsal and no matter how flashy your interpretation is, it's wrong and everybody knows it. It's a nice house, but nobody is home. A dead career.

So explore, reach for opposites, choose from the rich catalogue of human physical expression and pick the most dramatic way to communicate physically that emotional beat of your character. String them together, beat to beat, action to action from the beginning of the play to the end. Then you will have achieved your objective.

As you come upon various ways to physically manifest each beat, some will be discarded immediately while others you will want to explore. When you get it down to a few good choices, you have to feel them in your bones. That means that you must try them in rehearsal.

You might discard a few immediately. They *just don't feel right*. The rest, the few remaining choices, you must research with the body. See how they feel in your ankles, back, nose. Physically explore that emotional expression with your whole body. It's trial and error, check and re-check, trying to get it to feel good, look good, sound good. You must balance all three types of memory through rehearsal. But with proper rehearsal, you will get an always good, sometimes brilliant performance, while getting better everyday.

Professional methods lead to professional work. If the soul of acting is on the stage, the heart is always—by trade—in rehearsal. Never let it get boring. Explore, explode, expand, contract, take chances—work!

Just because you know the words doesn't mean that you can sing the song.

On Keeping it Fresh

An actress told me after she'd had a bad performance that she was burnt out on this piece of material. It was a workshop scene and she and another actor had worked on it over a two week period.

There is only one way that this can happen: *improper rehearsal technique.* I've done 150 performances of the same role and still managed to make exciting discoveries about my character on the night we closed.

Repeating yourself is dull. If that's all that you are doing in rehearsal you will burn out. Never do the same thing twice in rehearsal. Take chances and keep taking them right up to the point where you have to "set it" for the camera or a lighting effect on stage. Even then you can keep taking chances. You may have to be on your "mark" or down stage left, physically, but you can keep taking chances privately with your feelings: intensity levels and sensory stuff. In addition, if you have another actor to play with, look at him or her carefully. We are not the same every day. Sometimes you are tired, sick or riding an emotional high. Let some of that in.

Never feel that you know everything about your character.

You must understand that acting is fun work and if you let it get dull, you will be dull in your part. When it stops being fun, stop doing it. Realize how lucky you are to be an actor and always approach it with a sense of excitement and wonder.

A tip: usually more research into given circumstance will give you a fresh area to explore. The major difference between the amateur actor and the professional is in the amount and type of research.

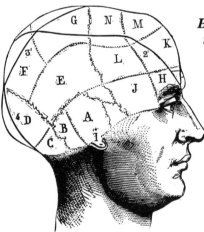

Balance all three types of memory through rehearsal

AFFECTIVE MEMORY

enerally, the best acting is done moment to moment—being there. You get your tears and laughter from complete involvement with the situation, from belief in your relationship with the other characters you're acting with. That's the best way. However, sometimes this is impossible. That is why Staniolavsky called his work, "For Those Moments of Difficulty."

In a play I was doing, I hit one of those moments. One of my scenes required that my eyes fill with real, live tears. I tried everything to get my tears from "the moment," but I could not. The tears *had* to be there, and on cue, too. So I went into my actor's tool bag and pulled out *affective memory*. Using this technique, I got the tears—on cue.

What is it? Well, sometimes actors have to fight to remember what all others fight to forget. By going back to a moment in your life when you were so saddened that tears flowed uncontrollably from your eyes, you can recreate that moment and cry again.

But according to Lee Strasberg, you should not use anything that is fresher than seven years old. There is a danger that emotional damage could result.

Don't go straight for the emotion. If you go for the emotion directly, it's like chasing a runaway puppy—the more you chase it, the further it gets away. If you stand still and call it softly, it will come to you.

Calling it softly in the case of affective memory means rebuilding the incident from the sensory elements of the situation, filling in every physical detail that you can remember:

> what you were touching,
> what you were smelling,
> what you were tasting,
> what you were seeing,
> what you were hearing,
> what you were wearing–right down to your
> underwear.

Most of this may be blocked, but take anything you do remember and start to build on it. Go slowly at first—it may take hours—but the tears will come. Eventually, you will get to the point when you can do it in minutes or seconds, depending on the needs of the scene. Go slowly. As details are remembered, they will call forth others.

Now the philosophy of this is something that everyone has to work out for themselves. The other night in my advanced workshop we were doing an affective memory exercise, and the actor in this case was willing to share his memory with us. He described in detail how his family waited around his grandfather's hospital deathbed for two hours. Since he was willing, I asked questions to fill in the gaps that he had left. There are no pleasant questions in a situation like this, and at one point I turned to the class and said, "Some of this may sound pretty ghoulish, but it is all necessary." I should add here that you do not need to tell anyone what you are using for an affective memory. That is your private property, and you need not let anyone in.

Later, I told the actor he obviously loved his grandfather, and that love was returned. He might think of the memory as the old man's last gift to him. Surely, were he alive, he would do anything to help the young man in what he had chosen as his life's work. In my own tragedy that I use night after night (and twice on Saturdays), I justify the use of the memory of someone I loved and who loved me by thinking that in some strange way they hear my thoughts and are happy to be thought of so warmly and lovingly, many years beyond the grave. I also believe that there is something sacred about the actor's art—but you don't have to go that far.

Crying, of course, is not the only emotion to get from this technique—you can get all of them this way. But it is hard work. There is an easier way and that is learning to believe the moment and your right to be there as that person.

The fact is that acting is a job. I might use the same effort to produce tears in a commercial about "my wife's bad coffee," when I can't get what I need by playing the moment. Affective memory is a powerful tool and the right tool at the right time gets the job done.

ON THE IMPORTANCE
OF SENSORY WORK

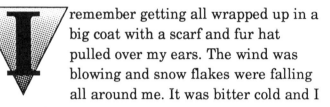remember getting all wrapped up in a big coat with a scarf and fur hat pulled over my ears. The wind was blowing and snow flakes were falling all around me. It was bitter cold and I was shivering so much that I thought I was going to shake myself to death. The director yelled, "Cut," and "Take a break." I quickly peeled off the coat, hat, gloves. I was soaked to the skin with sweat. The prop people were recycling the plastic snow flakes, the wind machine was off and many people were looking for a little piece of shade. It was mid-July and 115 degrees in Hollywood.

Make a list of 10 sensory situations you might be called on to create in a role. Five external (such as the one above), and five internal (for example, a drinking scene—if you were using real whiskey, you probably would not be able to walk or talk on cue).

The thing about sensory work is that it seems so difficult—if not impossible—that when you first encounter it you want to duck it. *Don't! Make the effort!* Tune in to yourself. You'll be astonished at the power of your own concentration.

Concentrate in the shower, feeling every little bead of water, where it hits, how it feels rolling down your body, the temperature. Feel the sun.

What part of your face is the hottest? Feel the difference from that part which is in the shade. Turn your face slowly. Concentrate on how the temperature changes. You will increase your sensitivity for all aspects of life.

As far as recreating these feelings on a cold sound stage or in the theater, it is not impossible. Now, neither I nor anyone else expects you to do this, but look at the extreme. There are guys in India who can stop their hearts, literally. They can also lower their body temperature 20 degrees or more. Seriously—this is documented.

It is all concentration. I am not going to sit on a mountain and hold my left arm out for twenty years just to prove I can, but this is what concentration can do. And an actor without concentration is like an Indy 500 driver without it—dead meat.

What happens when you lose concentration on stage or on the set is that you kill a big part of all the work all the people involved have put into making the production a success. You can create some real bad feelings when you do that. In movies and TV, where it costs thousands of dollars a minute to run a shoot—how popular are you going to be if you force extra takes because of poor concentration?

Exercise your sensory powers through a muscle called concentration, and you'll become more sensitive to the world around you and a better actor as well.

One more tip: Edward Easty's book *On Method Acting* can help you here.

ON BIO'S AND SYNOPSES

hen learning a scene, it is essential that you write a biography of your character and a short synopsis of the play. Make a detailed diagram of the setting, including the time, place, weather. When you see yourself in this environment, like a third eye, watch; then describe everything you do, giving dialogue when appropriate. Describe everything you hear, smell, taste and see. Make use of objects that have a personal value to you.

Synopses

Writing a synopsis can be invaluable if it is done from your character's point of view. It helps you find your character's objectives in each of your scenes, and your character's super objective, i.e. what your character wants from the total situation, the play or screenplay.

Write your synopsis in the first person: I this, I that, then I went, then I met, and we etc. Write not only your scenes, but what your character is doing when you're not on camera or stage. This will force you to visualize your character in a very clear, specific way as he or she starts, passes through and finishes the story. The Whelan Tape Technique mentioned earlier will feed and be fed by this work.

You will also make many discoveries which would have otherwise eaten up a lot of valuable rehearsal time. Remember, however, that that is the way you saw it. When you work with the other actors, the director and the producer, don't be surprised if they change it a little bit. But whether you keep some or none of what you visualized, you will have gained a great deal from the exercise. If you don't use any of it—and I have never seen any actor not use any at all—you will at least have learned not to do it that way. That may sound funny, but building a character is like a scientific experiment in that you try ideas against reality and when they don't work you have narrowed the possible ways of achieving your desired results.

Bio's

By writing a biography for your character, you start to build the chain of memories which will grow until your involvement with this character is completed.

As I said before, all characters have physical memories. Were they athletic as children, weak and inactive, or somewhere in between?

All characters have intellectual memories. Did they go to good schools, bad schools, or no schools at all? Did they read classical books or comic books or both?

They have emotional memories. Did they come from a loving family, were they abused as children, or what?

The biography is your major key to your character. It is the framework from which much of your research will grow.

Doing a part is a bit like putting together a big puzzle. After dumping all the pieces out on the floor, the first thing you do is look for corners and sides—the frame. Well, the puzzle that is your character has a framework, too. Given circumstance! From there, it's all imagination, but you must harness that imagination and make some basic choices to start with.

Don't get locked in. Well into rehearsal, you may decide that your character is really a Pisces, not a Virgo, born in New York, not Ohio. Take out your driver's license or other identification and look at it. Realize that your character has these things, too.

Be specific in your bio's. As part of your bio, do a year by year list of highlights of your character's life.

The most neglected word in the amateur actor's vocabulary is *research*.

ON ETHICS:
SEPARATING PROFESSIONAL
AND PRIVATE LIVES

here are many very good people in this business, but there are some not-so-good ones as well. You will work with both in the course of your career. You must never let your personal love, dislike or hatred of someone damage any production you are working on.

On the positive side: if you were a normal working person and you had one of these people in your office, you would have to deal with them for many years. In show biz, unless you're in a hit play that goes on forever, or a series, you are away from them quickly—after a few days on a commercial shoot, a week on a TV show, a month on a feature.

Although the length of time is short, the hours are long and the involvement intense. If you are going on location for six weeks in the mountains, the jungle, the desert, you can quickly see why complainers, snobs, and super-moody types are going to be unpopular and therefore uncast. These people will probably cause dissension somewhere along the line, and that is bad for morale. Morale is very important to a good shoot, and good shoots are what it is all about. Of course, the same applies to being cooped up in a theater for weeks of long days with the same people.

So if you are a tough-to-get-along-with-type, your first acting better be during the audition. Act like someone who might be fun or interesting to be locked up with in a small room for weeks. Don't walk in the door bitching about the audition time being too early, or too late, and they didn't give you enough time. Don't say that the coffee sucks, and don't ask why it is taking so long, or wonder loudly why the hell they didn't give you a script.

I hope you see the point, because it is *major*. Usually, if you can fake being a nice person until you get into production, people will adjust to you and you will probably complete the job. But, word gets around quickly—"She is such a pain in the ass to work with," or "He is such a stuck-up bastard, I hope that I never have to work with him again!"

You have a job to do and it does take a lot of concentration and privacy. Even though everyone around you is a pro, if they like you (the make-up and hair people, the lighting people, the wardrobe people) they will try a little harder to make you look better. If they, the so-called little people, are on your side, your job will be a lot easier. Never forget that acting is a collaborative art. You are not doing it alone. All of these people are necessary. If you cannot like some of them, you must respect all of them. If you don't, you're asking for trouble.

ON KEEPING
YOUR MOUTH SHUT

ou need an open mind in show business, or at the very least the ability to keep your politics and religion and social attitudes to yourself. Remember, this is a business. You don't go up to the president of IBM on a sales call and talk to him about God, your political views, or your sex life—not unless you've researched the man and you know what he wants to hear. But even then you take a chance—no one really knows what another believes. Someone's public posture can be a long way from what he believes passionately in his heart. Someone might be a Catholic, a Republican, a dog lover and a good father—for business reasons. But behind closed doors they are really a drug addicted, child molesting, commie Satan worshipper.

You are there to sell–

You the charming,

You the good looking

You the talented.

Don't get off the subject into gray areas that could hurt you. I actually heard an actor tell a casting agent that he thought her dress was ugly. I almost *died* from disbelief. He did not get that part, nor any other part *ever* from that lady.

Stars have outspoken views on politics and religion and that sort of stuff—*you don't!*

ON THE IMPORTANCE
OF IMPROVISATION

ore and more, today's directors, producers and casting agents are moving toward improvisations in casting and rehearsals. It is a necessary tool today for an actor approaching the marketplace—you will be asked to do it. So if you want to be competitive, learn it.

The advantage to directors should be obvious—he trusts that he will see more of your creativity in an improv than from you being tied to a script. You are free to move, use your feet, body, hands and eyes. Be inventive—he will probably give you an adjustment to see how you take direction. He might tell you to explore a creative avenue for his character, one that you had created up to that point. This can prove your worth—this is a creative exchange. The morality of his taking your input and then giving the part to somebody else—that's for the unions to decide. A good actor gives them what they want, *plus*.

Improvisation is not hard—for the most part, the work is already done. For as many years as you've been living, your mind-body-emotional memories have been storing everything and everybody and every place you've ever been, know or read. Whatever they ask you to do, somewhere in your mind you've got some little bit of information to start with. So just *jump in!* That is what they want you to do, so do it. Your willingness to try is the first thing they are looking for. The imagination shown by the choices you make is important too, but in this regard, don't second guess them. Follow your impulses, take chances, be bold. There's genius in boldness.

Tips—if none are given, create objects that relate to the character and space you're in (i.e., mime them). A gun, a car, a camera, a stove—whatever— these objects will sharpen the reality of *where* and *who* you are. Who and where are the first principles of improvisation, so invent objects and don't be sloppy with them.

Your willingness to jump in is the first thing they look for

ON LOOKING FOR WORK

hen it comes to pictures, the most important thing is that you are comfortable with the photographer. There are many good photographers out there and you must look at their work to make sure it's good, but after that it's all whether you feel comfortable with the photographer. If he or she makes you feel stupid or has an arrogant attitude, get out of there. No matter how famous or inexpensive the photographer is, if you're not comfortable you're wasting money. Pictures are still number one—you won't get in the door without a good one. Eight-by-ten-inch black & white shots are the best.

Very important—get a photo that looks like you. Don't be seduced by super glamor shots with dramatic lighting. When someone is casting and calls someone in from a photo, that person is who he wants to see walk in the door. Get one photo smiling and one not smiling. Use the smiling one for comedy and the serious one for dramatic roles.

Make sure you have an answering service or a machine. You can lose the part of your life by missing a phone call.

Video is really what's happening now. It means so much more when casting decision makers can actually see you walk and talk. It can be expensive, but most actors learn how to get expensive things at good prices. So start a video and add to it whenever you can.

Make a voice-over tape. There is a lot of work for voice people and the idea is to make a living as an actor, not as a waitress or an office temporary, so never miss a chance to make a buck as an actor. Voice-over work pays the rent and buys a lot of meals.

Most actors blow it because they don't realize that you not only have to build a better mouse trap, you have to sell it. You must always be working to be a better actor, but you also have to sell it. Follow ups are what sell—stay in their face! Also, get out and around. They (Decision Makers) are not out searching apartment buildings for new stars—but they do eat, shop, go to plays and movies and you can find out where. "They" were you before they made it. Don't bother people at dinner, however— just look as good as you can and be seen.

Agents

For a list of good agents, contact the unions (Screen Actors Guild or American Federation of Television and Radio Actors). For virtually pennies, they will give you a list of all "signators to the guild." That means that those on the list agree to treat actors according to union rules.

Send out pictures and resumes to those on the list. If you haven't done anything professionally, write a cover letter to go with your photo. Include all your sizes, height, weight, etc., any classes you've taken, school plays, special abilities, sports, foreign languages, glass-blowing—anything you can do. Be careful, though, if you put down glass blowing or sky-diving—be ready to do it!

Do a mailing to these agents, and after four days call and say you sent a picture and resumé (P & R) and did they get it and can you have an interview? If you get solid "no's" all around, you probably have a bad picture. Go get a new one and do it again. Don't argue or beg with these people—just keep finding new reasons to contact them: you got a part in a play, you have a new picture, whatever.

Life is better with an agent, but you still have to hustle. You are responsible for your own career at this stage, and an agent's value to you is mainly in being able to say you have one and in negotiating the contract for any work you get for yourself.

Getting work for yourself

The same books that have agents—Geographic Casting Guide, Ross Report, Studio Directory—have Casting Agents for TV shows, movies, etc. They also have producers and ad agencies. Send them all pictures and resumes and call them all up a few days later to ask for an audition or interview.

Again, stay in touch. I recently went back East to star in a feature film. I interviewed and did a tape audition for this film a year ago. The project got held up but I kept in touch—a card here, a phone call there—then one day the phone rings and I'm starring in a movie for 12 weeks, a great role and good money. I've received calls to do a TV project from a P & R I sent out six months before. Plant those seeds now!

Places to Look

Periodicals:

Los Angeles—
Dramalogue
Hollywood Reporter
Daily Variety
Weekly Variety

New York City—
Backstage
Show Business
Weekly Variety

Unions (Ask about the Players Guide):

AFTRA (American Federation of Televison & Radio Artists)
SAG (Screen Actors Guild)
AEA (Actors Equity Association)

Don't ignore the international situation—trans-Atlantic casting is on an upswing that should last forever. You can contact unions in other countries and ask about their trade papers.

Your audition video tape can get you a "call back" in another country.

If you're looking for a particular script, call one of
the major theatrical book stores. They will ship
directly to you if you have a major credit card:

Samuel French's Theater and Film Book Shop
7623 Sunset Blvd.
Los Angeles, CA 90046
213-876-0570
(also in New York at 212-206-8990)

Larry Edmund's Cinema and Theater Bookshop, Inc.
6658 Hollywood Blvd.
Los Angeles, CA 90028
213-463-3273

Drama Book Shop
723 7th Ave
New York, New York, 10019
212-944-0595

Applause Theater and Cinema Books
211 West 71st Street
New York, New York, 10023
212-496-7511

For experience, you can check out acting
opportunities in:
Cable Access Television
Student films at schools and colleges
Small Theaters

Libraries, both city and university, are one of the best sources of information—and you can't beat the price.

Some of the books you might read:

Boleslavsky — *The First Six Lessons*
Stanislavsky — *An Actor Prepares*
Building A Character
Creating A Role
Grotowski — Anything you can get your hands on
Spolin — *Improvisation for the Theater*
Brook — *The Empty Space*
Easty — *On Method Acting*
Shurtleff — *Audition*
Manderino — *All About Method Acting*
Benedetti — *Seeming, Being and Becoming*
Hagen — *Respect for Acting*
Logan — *Acting in the Million Dollar Minute*

THE VIEW FROM THE CREW

hat does a gaffer do? Or a key grip? Knowing what the crew is up to can help the cast turn in its best performance.

While playing the bad guy in a recent thriller, I asked various crew members during the shoot to describe what it is they do. Then I asked how actors can help them do it.

Take a look at the process through their eyes.

JIM HAYMEN, Director of Photography

"I would say that my position as DIRECTOR OF PHOTOGRAPHY (or DP) is basically one of being in control of the look and the visual style of the picture. I oversee the lighting, the choice of lenses, the framing, the camera movement—anything that really deals with the photographic/visual look of it.

"As far as what an actor can do to make my job easier, it leans more towards the technical end of the spectrum. One thing actors should remember is that no matter how good their performance is, if it isn't on screen, or in other words if it isn't in frame, it doesn't matter. So things as technical as hitting your mark for focus or hitting your light so you're correctly lit or exposed can make or break my job. I know it's a very difficult thing for an actor who comes from a stage background, or who plays off of more emotional stimuli, or a more method situation—they don't want to be bothered with that. But film's a very different medium. It really is a two-dimensional medium, and there is nothing more than light and shadows on the screen.

"Another thing that can help an actor is to understand their size in the frame and how to build an action or physicalize an action. If they are large in the frame, they need to bring the action down and play it smaller or softer or lower. If they are small in the frame, it has to be more physical.

"If they're in a close-up and they want to show an emotion it can be something as small as raising an eyebrow or a glance or a turn of the mouth or something like that.

"I guess the best way an actor can help me is to just try to involve themselves with my area of work. The more they're interested, the more they can trust me and understand that I'm seeing things that they're not, that I'm seeing their feelings. Now I'm not saying that I have control over what emotion they're presenting, but I see what is getting on screen and what isn't. Something as simple as 'How big am I in the frame?' can help their performance transpose from within to without. From inside them to on the screen.

"Generally, my job is to make actors look good, so the more that they listen to me the better they are going to look."

JOHN P. FINEGAN, Producer

"As a PRODUCER, I look for certain things in an actor, including the ability to grasp a part in short order and never stray from character. A good actor should also have the ability to be flexible while working with a director who may need to rewrite a scene on a moment's notice.

"Beginning actors need to develop professional habits from day one in this business."

WENDY ROBERTS, Script Supervisor

"My job is also called CONTINUITY SUPERVISOR and the primary thing that I do is oversee the continuity of a movie. Films are not shot in order. One scene or even part of a scene may be shot one day and then continued many days or weeks later. So, I keep track of many, many things.

"I usually work very closely with Wardrobe, Make-up and Props. It can be anything as boring as what ring goes on what finger or screen direction, which I find pretty interesting—working with the DIRECTOR and the DP to figure out how things should go together to make sense visually on the screen.

"A good example is if say an actor is walking down a street, has a newspaper under his arm, it is a rainy day and he goes into a bar. The outdoor scene may be shot in one day and maybe three weeks later, they'll shoot the inside view of him coming in the bar. When he comes in, he has to be wet, he has to have the exact same clothes on, the exact same make-up, the same newspaper folded in the same way under the same arm, collar turned up the same way, buttons on his coat the same way and he has to enter from the correct direction.

"I think the most difficult thing for an inexperienced film actor would be doing the exact same thing over and over again—hitting their marks, saying the same line with the same hand in their pocket. In film, it's absolutely essential that everything matches the master take. The close-ups, the medium shots, everything has to match it. I try to help the actors do the same things because it gives the EDITOR and DIRECTOR the most options. But sometimes it's a little difficult because there are so many things for everyone to concentrate on.

"Something actors should be aware of before they start shooting is that they are going to have to do the same thing over and over, exactly the same way. So their interpretation has to be thought of before hand, not while they're doing it.

"In my notebook I have all of the camera information, sound information, notes on every shot that has been shot, and notes from the DIRECTOR, the DP and anybody who asks me to take a note. I also have my own notes. For instance, here's a page on one of Kelly's scenes, saying her right knee is up, her right leg is behind the tire, her left hand is on the tire, the explosives are to her left. I have those kind of notes about actors, screen direction and so on. I'm really the only person who has that all in one place, so people come to me a lot to ask for information."

ANNE GWYNN, 2nd Assistant Cameraman

"Mainly my first responsibility is assisting the 1ST ASSISTANT CAMERAMAN, who is Geb. I do the slate, I keep camera reports, I load the film. On this job, though, we have a loader so I can spend my time on the set with Geb changing lenses, building the camera, and setting marks.

"When we do a shot, we lay down marks for the actors. That's my job to put the marks down. And doing the slate—take one, take two, take three, whether it's MOS (without sound). I keep all of the slate information and the camera reports on the back so that when we can out the film, that is, when it's shot and "in the can," there are reports that can go to the lab for the processing."

TOM RONDINELLA, Director, Co-writer & Editor

"My advice to actors as a WRITER is that there really is no advice I can give to actors, because writers are usually not involved in the actual production of a movie, they're mostly involved in the pre-production.

"As the DIRECTOR, what I ask of my actors is trust. Trust your director's decisions and what he sees, but also don't be afraid to make suggestions because it is a collaborative medium and the director listens to everybody. That includes the cast and the technical support people because there is no such thing as an *auteur* in filmmaking. It is a collaborative medium, so everyone has ideas, and everyone should be listened to—that's why you hire them.

"As an EDITOR, what I ask from an actor is that they repeat their actions the same way every time, and that they realize the power visually that a close-up has. They don't have to, let's say, be as broad in their actions in a close-up as they would be in a master shot. Also, continuity is very important because what makes an editor yell out in an editing room is when actors don't repeat the same actions or say the same dialogue as planned."

BILL PACE, Associate Producer

"Basically ASSOCIATE PRODUCER means anything, and nothing and everything in between. But it's a great job to have, and you can get it from sticking with the producer or you can get it from helping with the schedule.

"What do I need from actors? I like people to know their job, know how to work on a film unit, and still do their character work. And my advice to people? If you really want to do it, do it."

LAUREN MATENUS, Make-up Artist

"The job detail is to bring more character to the actor through make-up. This is primarily to bring out the highlights and shadows, so you give the actor a sense of security because he looks more like the character he's playing.

"The biggest problem with actors is when they think they know my job better than I do. But chances are the technician knows what he is doing, so trust him. If you know what works best on you, you may suggest it, but don't try to take over the process yourself."

CECILIA KATE ROQUE, Production Manager

"As the name implies, a PRODUCTION MANAGER manages the day to day operations of a movie production. This includes everything from monitoring the flow of money to cutting a deal for an out of town hotel to hiring the technical crew.

"I'm required to help reconcile the dreams of the director, writer and producer with the more tangible reality of the budget. Beyond being a problem solver, I feel it's also the PM's job to help keep the actors and crew happy in the sea of confusion that a shoot can sometimes become."

RICHARD AUDINO, 2nd Electrician

"The bottom line in film is overkill. You don't like to do things twice, so you do them incredibly seriously and really go overboard the first time around.

"The responsibilities of the 2ND ELECTRICIAN are to monitor electricity on the set, to make sure that the generator, if one is being used, operates properly, and to assist the GAFFER, who is the 1ST ELECTRICIAN.

"The actor—he or she—should always be aware of light, and blocking light. He should understand where the key light is at all times so that he can play to it. Crossing light, he should always be aware of his shadow, where his shadows are falling. When rehearsing, he should *always* perform the same way so that when the actual take happens, he doesn't miss his mark or miss his light, or whatever. There is obviously a lot more to this than lighting, but this is my specific department.

"For example, if he does his rehearsal one way— say he is crossing through a doorway and sits down at a table—we light for the rehearsal and when it comes time to actually take it, it's different and it ruins the effect. You can't do that.

"So basically, it sounds pretty machine-like. But that's how it should be because this is film and it's not a live medium, it's not changing. It's very plastic and it has to be able to be molded.

Author's note—This job is usually called BEST BOY. I've seen 60 year old Best Boys, as well as female Best Boys.

MARY BETH HAGNER, 1st Assistant Director

"The 1ST ASSISTANT DIRECTOR is the one on the set who always has to push the people to get the schedule done, and to hurry everybody up to shoot an impossible schedule on time, and on budget—sort of.

"I have no paper work, I give it all to my 2nd. In pre-production, I generally go over the shooting schedule. I do a strip board.

"When we're ready to roll, I say 'Roll sound,' and the Director says, 'Action.' And then he says, 'Cut,' and I repeat the 'Cut' into my walkie-talkie so everybody knows. Then I say, 'OK, now we're setting up over here, we have to move the trucks for a third time.'

"The only thing an actor can do to make my job easier, since I have nothing to do with performance, is just to basically be on time. That's really it. That's the whole thing. And be a nice person, and have a funny personality which all actors do anyway.

"They also can help make sure that all of the props go back to the Prop Department, and take off their wardrobe and give it back to Costume because it's very important for continuity. They shouldn't take anything into their own hands such as washing, taking off their own make-up, etc."

AMY LYNNE, 2nd Assistant Director

"A 2ND ASSISTANT DIRECTOR runs around, tells the Production Assistants (PA's) what to do, and handles background action and extras. She recharges walkie-talkies, she harasses a lot of people a lot of the time and she deals with Make-up and Wardrobe. I make sure that they're on time, and that the Talent is in and dressed and on the set on time. I also handle all paperwork from every department: Sound, Camera, Script.

"I am the AD's Assistant. It is also very important for my job as 2nd AD to lock-up background. 'Lock it up' means make sure that when we're rolling people aren't going through the background of our shot. Say we're shooting on a city street, I have to lock-up cars; here on the golf course I have to lock-up golfers.

"Another thing is total background action of the extras. Don't get lost. It is important that I know where people are. I work closely with the AD, and how many extras we have depends on the control of the background that I have."

MICHELE CLIFFORD, Wardrobe Supervisor

"My basic responsibilities are to take care of the costumes and make sure the actors get into their right costumes every morning. This includes doing laundry, and things of that nature or seeing that it's done. I was also responsible for acquiring the costumes and making sure that they fit everyone. If clothes have to be bloodied or dirtied or greased up in any way—ripped or torn—it's my job to take care of it. If they are ripped or torn and they're not supposed to be, it is my job to fix them. It is also my job to check the actors before every take and make sure their costumes are right. That is, to make sure that collars are out if they are supposed to be, wrinkles are not there if they're not supposed to be and things of that nature.

"What an actor can do to help me is basically be cooperative, as far as getting into what they're supposed to get into and not being fussy about things. I mean, the Director knows what you're supposed to look like and you may think you have an idea, but maybe it's not actually the way it should be. Just cooperation and doing what's asked of you or answering questions is the best way to help. Providing accurate sizes is also very important. What you may think you are or what you think you may be after you lose five pounds is not what to give for sizes. I need exactly the sizes that you are, so that you can be measured and fitted properly. That's about it, really. Cooperation is just the best thing. Not being a fuss-budget is the most important factor, as far as I'm concerned."

SEAN GILBERT, Electrician

"Basically we're responsible for lighting. In my end of the department, we run the power and do the actual focusing and rigs and things like that.

"We're on set almost all of the time. And besides just doing the actual lighting, there are times when I feel that the department is something like the pulsebeat of the set because we're always there, and in many ways we're able to keep the tempo going.

"In terms of what an actor can do, it's more just a matter of knowing and being aware of what it is that we're doing, and how it can relate to them.

"The thing that I would like actors and actresses to know is that the crew is made up of people just like them. Sometimes my favorite thing is just to hang out with an actor or an actress, and just have a cigarette or a cup of coffee and to know that we are all just people. We are all in it together. Sometimes, I feel that when we all start out, everybody feels a little bit distanced, you know, particularly because an actor or an actress is kind of shuttled in and then shuttled back out again, and they even feel it's a little difficult for them to feel at ease with everybody. But the crew feels more of an affinity for people when everybody can kind of say, 'Hello' to each other and just know they're all in it together."

ED McAVENY, Assistant Art Director

"My position is technically ASSISTANT ART DIRECTOR, but I'm actually wearing more hats than that. I'm the SET DECORATOR, PROPERTY MANAGER, and MASTER CARPENTER. So that's building all of the sets, decorating all of the sets, and handling all of the props.

"Now, for an actor, the most important thing prop-wise is, remember where things are and where they belong. When we do takes and we have to cut away, or we do overlapping action so that it matches, we need to use a specific cutting point for editing. You have to remember what hand you picked things up with and exactly where you put them down.

"So the best thing for an actor is to remember all of those little details of where set pieces are. They should familiarize themselves with the set before they come on it to shoot, so they know where everything is, where they can move in the space and just be aware of their surroundings and play off of it."

J.C. SVEC, Production Designer

"Basically and simply, what I am responsible for is the complete, total and overall look of the movie, meaning Props, Wardrobe, Sets, and on a low budget film even into Special Effects, Prosthetics, etc.

"What I would love for an actor to do for me is once they are cast and once we are introduced, or once they know who the Production Designer is, to make available time so we can discuss special needs they might have for personal props—problems they may have with certain materials that can be related to Wardrobe, and just nice discussion dealing with how they may look or what their surroundings are going to look like.

"It is good for me to see the actors initially to see their skin tones, and for me to get an idea of their sizes, in comparison to other actors and actresses. This usually helps with color coordination and to make sure we can fit them into an environment they will be comfortable in and that will be best for the overall look of the picture.

"Knowing about special little prop requirements helps, because then I can fit that into the budget and into shopping.

"It is always good for them to have an idea of how things are built, how things are going to be built. Once they step on the set, they should know what their environment is made of, so that they don't cause damage to it or to themselves."

BRIT WARNER, Location Audio Mixer

"My responsibilities include the quality of all of the audio that is recorded on location. I help place the microphones, consider the microphone techniques and the type of mikes used, whether it's boom, or wireless, or hard wire, or planted mikes. I also listen very closely to the way actors deliver their lines, for dynamics, correct speech, if they flub words or whatever. I'm in communication with the Director. I discern whether it's good, bad, indifferent, or if there are background noise problems. I work very closely with the BOOM OPERATOR, of course. Also with the Gaffer and the Director of Photography. Once the Gaffer gets his lights set and the DP gets his shots set, then I usually have to decide how and where my mikes can work and how they're utilized.

"The most critical thing in Audio, in my opinion, is mike placement, and utilization of proper miking techniques. It really doesn't matter what all of the other equipment does if the mike is not in the right place to hear the actor. The actor on his part should strive for concise delivery, emotion in the voice, and proper dynamic delivery. This always makes the audio more interesting. Some actors I've worked with are very monotone. It removes some of the presence of their character, at least in my opinion. Obviously, it's a priority with me. They might look good on film, but if they don't sound good they could end up with someone else's voice being looped in. So give the audio guy a little credence—he knows what he is doing."

GEB BEYERS, Assistant Cameraman

"The major responsibility of the ASSISTANT CAMERAMAN is pulling focus. If an actor realizes exactly what the lenses do to his actions, that's probably the most important thing to help me in my job. The tighter the lens, the closer we get to the actor optically, the less the depth of field and the more critical the focus.

"My job is basically to keep the action in focus. That can be very difficult, especially with tight lenses or longer lenses. So when marks are put down, it is very important that the actor follows his marks because that's the only reference spatially that I have.

"It is a very archaic system. I see the mark on the floor, I know exactly where you are in the lens. Obviously action changes, but once it is set, it is important to try to hit one's marks. Hopefully, the focus-puller will make adjustments if the actor doesn't hit it.

"Especially on very tight lenses, keeping actions deliberate and not trying to introduce something new also helps the focus. If the focus-puller is aware of an action, such as getting up from a chair and moving, it makes a great deal of difference."

WILFRED CABAN, Special Effects Man

"My responsibilities include Pyrotechnics and the radio-controlled lawn mower on this picture.

"As far as what actors can do for me, the main things are to listen, to hit their marks, and to have a general idea as to what is involved between myself and the STUNT COORDINATOR. It's pretty much just a question of hitting your mark and seeing exactly what's in front of you, as far as effects are concerned."

MARK H. WILKINS, Boom Operator

"Operating the boom which holds the microphone, I have to be very aware of any volume changes the actors are using. Because the mike is actually the acoustic ear that hears what the camera sees.

"The boom moves with the talent. Lavalier microphones, on the other hand, are for more static situations. There are a wide variety of techniques and microphones and special-use implements such as wind screens, etc.

"To actors, the best thing I could tell you is to keep your volume level exactly the same when tape and film are rolling as they were in rehearsal. The Boomer gets in as close as he needs to to set recording levels. However, if your level changes between the time of rehearsal and the time we shoot, it could cause a re-take.

"Consistency in your audio level is greatly helpful to your career as an actor. Consistency is the name of the game."

ROB PAGLIARO, Craft Services

"My job is to provide the food, snacks and refreshments, and most of all coffee for the cast and crew on the set.

"The easiest thing you could do to make me happy is just to not complain about the food. Just eat whatever I give you, and understand that I am doing everything in my power to make you happy, even if it doesn't look that way.

"Also, pick up your trash."

BILL TAYLOR, Key Grip

"The job of the KEY GRIP is to run all of the GRIPS, and be responsible for all of the camera movements, safety, rigging and light control. On smaller films, such as this one, he pushes the dolly (a small camera platform on wheels). On larger films, there is usually a DOLLY GRIP.

"I like to think my primary function is to stand back from all of the excitement and direct the boys. My primary function does have to do with safety. You have a lot of big equipment and heavy lights that have to be put in a lot of difficult places, and you have to stand back and take an overall view of things. You have to do it quickly, safely, and be able to take whatever rigs or whatever you're doing down quickly.

"My advice to young actors starting out is to realize that film is a technical artform, and there are a lot of people involved in a lot of potentially dangerous situations with lights and equipment.

When you are all wrapped up in your part, sometimes it's easy to forget there are a lot of big pieces of equipment around you. Also, the boys are running around lifting things and it is courteous to get out of their way and let them get by if you can.

"I don't think an actor should ever have to touch a piece of equipment. Even though you see the grips doing things and you might want to give a hand, just stand back and let them do it because a lot of these things work in different ways than they appear to, and you could get hurt.

"It is very important to hit your marks all of the time, because the AC would love to get you in focus. It helps the cameraman, and it helps the dolly grip follow you. So it is always very important to do the same action time and time again, so everyone can follow you."

CHRISTY HOPKINS, Office Production Assistant

"The job of the Production Assistant is explained elsewhere. But working as the OFFICE PRODUCTION ASSISTANT allowed me not only to go to the set and learn what happens there, but also to learn about the inner workings of the office. There is much more to production than meets the eye. Once the filming is completed, the film and sound tapes must be gathered, logged, labeled, and sent to be processed.

"Every actor and actress should know some of the other aspects of the business in order to understand the mechanics and technicalities involved. And starting at the bottom of the ladder as a PA is a wonderful opportunity to learn."

TONY CUCCUARI, 2nd Unit Director of Photography

"My responsibilities are to continue those scenes or shots that the 1ST UNIT was unable to complete or get to. It often means having to pick up an action or to get an insert, a close-up, of something that was started another time in another place, so I've got to recreate what was done.

"In terms of acting, it means that an actor should be able to remember what he was doing, what his action was and other continuity details, such as in which hand he was holding something, what he was wearing, which way he was looking. Eye direction is very important.

"As time passes people forget, confusion ensues, and then in the cutting room it doesn't quite match. The work doesn't work. So remembering—keeping things straight—is extremely important.

"And again, a general note about acting for the camera—it's in the eyes and the face."

EDGARD MOURINO, Stunt Coordinator

"My duties are to hire STUNT MEN who double for actors. At times I work with the actors themselves, to teach them and coach them when they have to perform stunts. I am also the SAFETY COORDINATOR, where I oversee all safety procedures.

"I work in close contact with the Director and the Director of Photography and the Producers in order to put together the stunts I am supposed to design or figure them out as safely as possible for everyone concerned.

"Often when I read a script, I suggest where stunts may be needed or how elaborate they should be. I survey potential locations and advise on the execution of stunts. I hire the stunt men I feel are the most capable or best suited to do the work. I also obtain the necessary equipment, I choreograph the stunts, and I coach the stunt men.

"My advice to an actor is if he wants to get involved in the action, he should first go and learn more about it. If he doesn't, then on the set he should always depend on a Coordinator and not put himself in jeopardy by trying to perform stunts that he doesn't know how to do. There's more to it than you can see. When working with a Coordinator, the actor should completely rely on the Coordinator when stunts are being filmed."

BILL HAGEN, Production Assistant

"There were six different PRODUCTION ASSISTANTS and each had a different job. One PA, Dan, would be a runner. He'd run the dailies (the film shot that day, ready to be processed) back and forth to New York. Then there was Bill McDevitt. He was a Production Assistant but he worked with the Grips, pretty much as an apprentice. I was lucky, I got to work with every department, including the ART DEPARTMENT. I did whatever was needed, getting gasoline, picking people up, picking up one of the many broken cars at John's Auto Body. I worked with the Grips setting up different lighting. Or I worked with the Electrician with the cables. I pretty much assisted everyone on the set. I was even able to jump in as an extra a couple of times.

"In the morning, I assisted in driving people to the set, getting gas for the generator, smokes, etc. I assisted everyone including the actors if they needed something.

"As far as an actor helping a PA, just be nice and polite without giving him a hard time because he's only trying to do his job. It is a good experience, especially in my position because I was able to work with every department and learn exactly what job every department is doing."

DAVE WHITNEY, 2nd Grip

"It's my job to put shadows and darkness wherever the Director of Photography wants them. And it's also my responsibility to make sure that things are safe on the set. If that means tieing something down on a windy day or just making sure that nobody trips on a twig, it's being responsible for safety.

"If I had a suggestion for an actor, it would be to just act, and that's it. I'd like to thank you very much. I'd like to thank the Director, and the Producer..."

RICK LUDWIG, 1/2 Grip & 1/2 Electrician

"I'm the SWING between the Grip and the Electric Department. My job is to serve both the electricians and the grip department as a go between, where I have to know electrical work and grip work.

"Usually on a low budget film, they have a couple of Swing guys and PA's who help out. Mostly the job involves rigging, lighting, storing the equipment, safety, things like that."

ANDREA DORMAN, 2nd Assistant Cameraman

"My jobs consist of loading raw film stock into magazines to be loaded into the camera by the 1st Assistant Cameraman, and unloading exposed stock into a can to be processed by the lab. I also take care of slating (that famous moment when the camera films the chalkboard with the sticks that clap together to enable the editor to match up picture and sound).

"At the end of the day, I'm also responsible for inventorying the amount of exposed film as a total and comparing that number to the amount of unexposed film that we have ordered or bought for the shoot. So, basically my responsibilities are with the film. I am basically the film monitor.

"My job is done well if there are no negative or base scratches in the film, if the film is clean, and if it gets to the lab in good condition and it's unloaded carefully and safely.

"That inventory is given to the Production Office and we hope they're happy with the numbers—that the numbers coincide with their numbers. The film is slated correctly for the EDITOR so that he can match picture and sound. And that is my responsibility.

"My job has nothing to do with actors. Actors are nice people and we get along fine, but nothing an actor does has any effect on my job. I don't have any direct dealing with any actor. I am a supporting member of the CAMERA CREW."

BRIAN GREENBAUM, Production Office Coordinator

"The PRODUCTION OFFICE CORDINATOR is responsible for all the logistics of business between the set and the outside world. This entails ordering production supplies and rental equipment, vehicles necessary for their transportation, and coordinating personnel on "runs".

"It is the Production Coordinator's realm to find those strange requests at odd hours. The Coordinator is also responsible for the production office and for creating a paper trail for both the current production communication, and as a record of production. This paper work includes, daily call sheets, script notes, production reports, purchase orders, camera reports, memos. Finally, the Production Coordinator serves as a focal point of communication, ensuring that all parties necessary to a production have the information and paperwork they need to function.

"What can an actor do to make my life easier? One thing is, always realize whose jurisdiction you're under. When you're not on set, let the Coordinator know where you're going to be.

"Let the office know what your telephone number is. If you've got different transportation than usual, just keep the information flowing. And understand as an actor, you are a principal asset of the film. We have to know where you are, how to reach you, and anything that's changing in your schedule."

SCOTT BUCKLER, Gaffer

"I'm responsible for the lighting and the look of the film in accordance to what the CAMERAMAN is looking for. I talk to the Cameramen and sometimes even the Director about what the look of the film will be—what is necessary. Sometimes it's simply technical—it's daytime or it's nighttime. Or sometimes it's meant to convey an aesthetic feeling—happy, moody, somber, whatever.

"I translate the Cameramen's desires and needs into the actual technical information for the Crew to follow. So I'm a liaison between the creative departments—the Cameramen and the Director, and the Crew. In my case, I'm also supplying equipment. I'm known as an OWNER/ OPERATOR—there are a great number of Gaffers who are owner/operators. I have the added responsibility of supplying all of the equipment and having all of the necessary items for carrying out creative and technical needs for the movie.

"For this film, I'm also the designer for the rigging equipment. I designed various rigs to meet the needs of the creative aspects of the film, and provide the technical means for carrying them out.

"Now as far as actors are concerned, my advice is to be conscious of lighting. I would even recommend that actors acquire some technical knowledge of what fixtures do what, because soft light works differently than hard light.

"Many times these lights are set for specific positions, and if an actor hits his mark, he looks very nice. If he doesn't hit his mark, he's going to look bad. You're not in your own realm. You're not just acting for the Director, you're acting for the Director in a photographic medium. This means that the lighting that falls on you is equally as important as the acting that you're doing.

"Sometimes in certain lighting set-ups, you may be asked to look a certain way or hold an exact position for lighting, and it's really meant that way. If you don't hold that position, that take won't be good. And say that take has a great acting performance and another take you did hit the lighting just right, but has a bad acting performance. Either way, you're going to look bad. So, you're either going to be seen in bad lighting or bad acting for whatever take is used in the movie.

"What you're looking for is to have good acting occur at the same time as good lighting. We all look good when you guys look good."

A HANDFUL OF LOOSE NOTES

cting is like driving a car. The basics are simple and limited:

You have to:

    start it • stop it

    steer it, and • shift its gears.

You must also keep your concentration or you endanger yourself and others.

Although thousands of books and millions of pages have been written on how to act, acting has certain basic rules. If you learn *them*, you're home.

I really don't want to push the analogy too far, although you could say how at first you drive awkwardly, trying to integrate the various functions, and later you jump in and roar off. Acting is exactly the same. If you love it—acting or driving—you go pro. This means that you perfect your basic skills and then take concentration to its highest (life or death) level. The key is concentration.

Shifting gears is the most technically demanding of all the aspects of driving. I've no knowledge of any professional race driver who uses an automatic shift. They may do it so smoothly that it *seems* automatic, but they concentrate fully on every shift. It is the same with acting. Now shifting gears is not more important than steering. Likewise, changing

Acting is like driving a car

emotions is no more important than knowing where you are in relation to the stage or camera.

There is a technique to shifting;

A technique to steering;

A technique to changing emotion; and

A technique to awareness of where you are.

These techniques are simple and few. They are at once easy to understand and difficult to perform. *Practice:* the conscious application of technique through the discipline of perfect concentration.

It Takes Courage To Be An Actor

Everyone has an ego, and most would rather die than surrender it. They will fight with whatever tools are available to protect it. They will defend it and admire it, that little bit of individuality which makes them unique. To be someone else, to act a role, is to relinquish your ego. To have someone else's ego is frightening. If you are strong and your character is weak, it will take courage to enter into the heart of a coward. If you are religious, it will take courage to give up your God, if the part calls for it. Our goal is not to *act* the part, but to be the part, to enter into its heart and soul. It takes courage to let old attitudes and habits go, to think the way someone else thinks.

If It Doesn't Make Sense To The Actor, It Will Never Make Sense To The Audience

So much of the actor's problem is understanding what his character is saying. The way to cure this is to say every line of dialogue as *you* would say it. Even if it is obvious, even if what you would say is close, *do it*. Translate it into Youanese—your own language—and then you understand it. Then it is totally real to you.

On Subtext

Subtext is a method technique, but it is also something that any actor should have realized for himself. I can draw an example from the play I recently completed, "Watch on the Rhine." There was a moment when Fanny says to Tech (my character) that she had heard about my winning some money in a poker game with some Nazis at the German Embassy. I had not really connected with the moment until I realized what the dramatic implications of the statement were.

Originally I was working on bigger moments in the play and had considered this moment a "throw-away." But as I started to come together with the major moments of the character, my mind was free to investigate moments that had been ignored.

As soon as I took the time to think about it, I realized how significant this statement was. If Fanny knew what I was really up to, then I had to do something—fast. But if she knew of the poker game as only a little piece of gossip, then I was ok.

Tech had to study Fanny's face as she said this, looking for clues in her eyes and listening for them in her voice. I was talking to myself, "How much do you know, Fanny? Do you know about the list? Do you know your son in law is a German outlaw? What do you know? How far are you going to take this right now?"

All of a sudden, a moment that I originally thought was unimportant became a life or death situation.

The talking to myself was subtext. Simply put, it's what you're thinking while you're listening to, or talking to, someone else. So don't get caught just waiting. Think about what your character is thinking while other people are speaking to him.

Take What You Get

Sometimes, you and someone you're working with may be at different levels of training. If you're doing a Hollywood film, you may have spent 20 years at the Old Vic, and the heroine might be some girl the director saw at a bus stop. But you're going to have to act with her, and she with you.

Use Your Script

Write on it. Jot down your ideas for props, costumes, what's beyond, environment, sounds, smells, etc.

Stay In The Scene

If you lose your concentration, get it back. It will happen but you must train yourself *now* to grab yourself by the throat and force yourself back into character, back into the scene you are working on. This discipline is one of the most important aspects of your growth.

You are always:

A) *Coming from somewhere*—you bring some of that into each new place

B) *Somewhere*—you have to play the place you're in

C) *Going somewhere*—play the anticipation

We are never static. We are the result of our history and the energy of our dreams.

Index

About The Author

Jeremy Whelan has been a working actor for most of the last 30 years. He's studied with some of the legendary masters. He's acted alongside superstars.

Since his work has encompassed so many aspects of show business—from off-Broadway plays to dinner theater, from tv commercials to feature films—he's uniquely qualified to speak to the up and coming actor.

Between roles in recent years, he's conducted seminars and workshops on both coasts, giving hundreds and hundreds of newcomers the practical training they need for success in an acting career.

He currently lives in Philadelphia.

©1990 Mike Nathaniel Welch

Order Form

Please send me _____ copies of *The ABC's of Acting (The Art, Business and Craft)* at $10.95 each. I understand I may return the book(s) undamaged for a full refund if not satisfied.

Name _____

Address _____

_____

City _____ State ____ Zip _____

Phone (_____) _____

Shipping:
Add $1.50 for the first book and 50¢ for each additional book. If you can't wait three to four weeks for Book Rate delivery, add $2.50 per book for Air Mail.

Send order to:
Grey Heron Books
290 SW Tualatin Loop
West Linn, OR 97068

Thank you.

Order Form

Please send me _____ copies of *The ABC's of Acting (The Art, Business and Craft)* at $10.95 each. I understand I may return the book(s) undamaged for a full refund if not satisfied.

Name _____

Address _____

_____

City _____ State ____ Zip _____

Phone (_____) _____

Shipping:
Add $1.50 for the first book and 50¢ for each additional book. If you can't wait three to four weeks for Book Rate delivery, add $2.50 per book for Air Mail.

Send order to:
Grey Heron Books
290 SW Tualatin Loop
West Linn, OR 97068

Thank you.